PREPP

How to Develop Situational Awareness the Way
the Us Military Does

(Prepare Now to Survive Mother Nature's Wrath
or Mankind's Madness)

Minnie Medina

Published by John Kembrey

Minnie Medina

All Rights Reserved

Prepper: How to Develop Situational Awareness the Way the Us Military Does (Prepare Now to Survive Mother Nature's Wrath or Mankind's Madness)

ISBN 978-1-77485-121-0

Legal & Disclaimer

The information contained in this book is not designed to replace or take the place of any form of medicine or professional medical advice. The information in this book has been provided for educational and entertainment purposes only.

The information contained in this book has been compiled from sources deemed reliable, and it is accurate to the best of the Author's knowledge; however, the Author cannot guarantee its accuracy and validity and cannot be held liable for any errors or omissions. Changes are periodically made to this book. You must consult your doctor or get professional medical advice before using any of the suggested remedies, techniques, or information in this book.

Upon using the information contained in this book, you agree to hold harmless the Author from and against any damages, costs, and expenses, including any legal fees potentially resulting from the application of any of the information provided by this guide. This disclaimer applies to any damages or injury caused by the use and application, whether directly or indirectly, of any advice or information presented, whether for breach of contract, tort, negligence, personal injury, criminal intent, or under any other cause of action.

You agree to accept all risks of using the information presented inside this book. You need to consult a professional medical practitioner in order to ensure you are both able and healthy enough to participate in this program.

Table of Contents

Introduction

This book contains proven steps and strategies on how to begin setting up your Family Emergency Preparedness plan.

As a culture, we are used to preparing for accidents or other unpredictable events. We buy homeowner's insurance, car insurance and health insurance just in case. It gives us peace of mind knowing we have a safety net just in case something does go wrong. Although nobody wants to be in a car accident or have their water pipes burst and flood their homes, there is a certain sense of "everything is going to be okay" when you have a nice insurance plan to whip out.

This type of insurance is what drives some people to prepare to handle a disaster. You don't have to be the kind of person who digs giant holes and plants massive containers in to hide in if there is trouble, but you can create a nice insurance plan by having some things stored away for a rainy day so to speak. Because we just never know when things are going to go awry, having a backup plan that includes food, water and medical supplies for the family just makes sense. You don't have to be the stereotypical prepper to prepare for an emergency.

This book will help guide you in creating a plan for your family to follow in case disaster strikes. Keep in mind; disaster doesn't always come in the form of Mother Nature's wrath. It could be anything from a family member getting extremely ill or somebody losing their job and the family budget is cut in half. Disaster can come in many different shapes and sizes. It is always best to be prepared for whatever may come your way.

You will sleep better at night and likely feel less stress in general. How many nights have you lain awake wondering how you would put food on the table if you or your spouse lost your job? Knowing you have a backup plan can help you relax and enjoy the good times knowing the hard times won't be so bad with your well-stocked supply kit.

Chapter 1: How To Start Prepping

Here are some questions to ponder about prepping.

Are you preparing financially?

Are you preparing for doomsday?

Are you preparing for a military invasion?

Do you want to protect your family?

Are you preparing for other emergency scenarios?

There is so much money you can spend on prepping, but you'd need to direct your focus to what exactly you are preparing for, and what you can afford financially. Here you would appreciate the community setting of prepping; you could find different people preparing for things entirely different from yours, and they become a potential companion in the event of a disaster.

Irrespective of the different reasons for our preparation, there is a common ground denoted by the basic needs of every person. The needs include:

Food

Medical experts estimate the human ability to survive without food to be three weeks, at maximum. As preppers, food supply is indispensable to survival; depending on the nature of the emergency, you may be needing a lot of energy supply to thrive.

A rule of thumb for preppers is that you are required to store food, but a little guidance would be required when it comes to storing food. You wouldn't want to store food you can't consume, cook, or would get spoilt in storage.

Preppers usually give priority to food items that do not require refrigeration and possess a longer shelf life. Generally, preppers store food to last for at least two weeks. Obviously, the quantity of food stored varies from individual to individual depending on the average calorie count.

Some preppers choose to grow certain types of food so they can be easily available during emergencies. It is also crucial to note that the food stored must be ready to eat or easy to cook by unconventional means. Preppers may consider the difficulties in accessing gas or electricity in a disruption. One popular class of food items among preppers is food bars, as they contain high energy compounds. They would come in handy during emergencies, without taking up too much space in your stockpile.

Water

If I were to order this list according to priority, water ranks higher than food. Medical experts estimate a maximum of three days to survive without water.

By all means possible, you must find innovative means of storing pure water; one such means is a water filter. A water filter decontaminates and ensures a store of pure water is easily facilitated.

Air

Preppers try to avoid any shortage of air supply. Air ranks high above food and water because three minutes of its absence means certain death. Artificial store of air is the only way to prepare for emergencies that may affect air quality. Gas masks could be purchased to prepare for this scenario. While there are very few disasters that affect air supply, the goal of prepping is to prepare for the worst.

The three subjects discussed form the common ground all preppers share with regards to prepping. Having established this common connection, how do you start prepping?

Ascertain Your Reason for Prepping

This is the first step when you want to start prepping. The preparation and financial cost involved in preparing against an apocalypse cannot be compared to a preparation to survive food and water scarcity. Take a pen and a journal, and note down why have you decided to start prepping.

Take note of Common Needs

There is no prepping without the essentials for survival (food, water, shelter, security). You can store only water and food, but arrangements can be made for shelter and security.

Create an Itemized List

Having defined your reason you would need to identify what you would need to prepare. If you are preparing against a possible food shortage, you would need your food journal to identify what items to stockpile according to calorie counts. If you are preparing to strengthen your defense you would need to list down some equipment, self-defense skills and other factors related to your preparation.

Act Upon Your List of Preparations

Act out your preparations immediately. Do you need to stockpile more food, or purchase some survival kits? You should also start acquiring relevant skills and equipment.

Make Plans for Evacuation and Emergency

Make plans for evacuation; most preppers have a bug out bag in case they need to evacuate urgently. These bags contain enough to supply and sustain them during the crisis. With regard to an emergency, you would need to have plans for reaching loved ones immediately and evacuating them from the area of crisis. Other emergency plans range from cash, identifications, relevant medical records to possible locations to get help.

Prepping is Better Off as a Lifestyle

Prepping does not stop once you are done procuring the items in your list. Prepping as a lifestyle is more beneficial, as there could be emergencies or factors that you did not account for initially. Try to join a prepping community or establish one of your own. This way, you are always prepared and able to call out for additional help. A good place to start is by getting family members, co-workers and friends interested in prepping, especially if you live alone.

Chapter 2: Shelter & Clothing Preparedness

When disaster strikes, you may find yourself in a situation where you are exposed to the different elements of weather. If you are exposed to extreme cold, you may die of hypothermia (a situation where you are exposed to dangerously low body temperature) if you don't have a heat source (body heat or fire), insulation (from ground, rain, wind and air), or are near a location that poses any danger. And if you are exposed to extremely high levels of heat, you could die of heat loss. This means that you will need to prep for how you will survive in either of the two extremes. Remember that you can only stay alive for about 3 hours if you don't have synchronized body temperature.

Shelter preparedness means that you need to prepare for making a shelter anywhere once you evacuate your home or are forced to leave it when disaster strikes. It encompasses 'shelter-in-place' and 'evacuation preparedness'; these two will be discussed in depth in the later chapters. Right now, we are going to focus on how you can prepare for making a shelter out in the wild.

You need to stock the following items in your bug out bag for making a warm shelter anywhere once you abandon your house.

Sleeping Bags: You need subzero sleeping bags; it is best to get two sleeping bags per person. Any zero rated bag should be enough to give you enough warmth even at temperatures below zero. If you are in a region around desert, you should understand that such areas may often get to extremely low temperatures at night so you shouldn't just assume that just because you are prepping for extreme heat, you don't need anything for extreme cold. There can come situations when you are forced to leave your in-use sleeping bag out in the open because of a wild animal, any predator, or a disaster, or your sleeping bag gets destroyed. If you have another bag, you can use it in that situation.

Bivvy: You need to stock at least two Mylar blankets or bivvy per person. They are also referred to as survival blankets by preppers. They are good for keeping you warm in the cold, for protecting you against fire breakouts and you can spread them on the ground to sleep on it.

Fire Starters: You must store fire starters, such as lighters, matches, or flint bars. It is best to stock all these three fire starters. Keep at least 50 boxes of matchsticks, 60 to 70 lighters and about 50 flint bars. Ensure to keep a convex lens to improvise fire lighting just in case your matchsticks don't work (you simply concentrate sun rays on tinder until the tinder starts smoldering). You should also ensure that you learn numerous ways of lighting fire like using a metal match, flint, and steel, and fire plow since these may come in handy at different situations post disaster. Fire starters are important because you can use them for lighting up a fire and keeping yourself warm. Staying warm is important to combat hypothermia which is a condition wherein your body temperature becomes critically low. This condition can even put you at the verge of death, so you MUST stock fire starters. Also, they help you cook food easily.

Note: Don't use rocks that you obtain from the river to act as base for lighting a fire since these may explode when heated due to the extra moisture that they may have. The rocks may as well have some air pockets, which may cause them to explode when you expose them to heat. Therefore, ensure to set up the fireplace away from your shelter (at a safe distance).

Lighting Tools: You must also store about 50 to 70 flashlights, headlamps and lanterns each, so you can find your way easily in the dark. Make sure to store an abundant supply of batteries, specifically ones that are solar powered. You must also keep about 10 to 20 hand cranks, so you can recharge batteries with ease.

Rope: Keep about 200 meters of good quality rope, so you can use it for building shelters by lashing tree branches, making traps, and for crafting survival tools like spears. It is best if you invest in Paracord as it is sturdy, durable, light, and multifunctional.

Survival Knives: Keep at least 30 good quality survival knives that can help you cut wood, rope and several other objects easily for making a shelter. Also, they come in handy when you are attacked by animals or other people.

Tents: You should try keeping equipment and supplies for making at least five tents.

Each of the tents should be big enough to accommodate at least 10 people at a time.

Important Tools: Though, the aforementioned tools are good enough to help you prepare and manage your shelter, it is best you invest in a few more tools as well. This list includes hammer, saws, axe, pliers, wedge, and measuring tape. It is best to stock two of each of these tools. These can help you cut wood and various objects easily, attach them to sturdy supports and help you create a reasonable shelter for you. Do store an ample supply of duct tape to fasten and attach things easily in the hour of need. You must keep a compass and a map in your bug out bag, so you know which direction you are heading in and can find a safe spot easily. Also, stock two to three mirrors of different sizes for signaling for help.

It is essential that you; learn how to set up tents; learn how to properly use a sleeping bag; learn how to efficiently use each of the tools mentioned above; cut wood using a knife and prepare a shelter using branches and rope. If you have a backyard or a garden, or can go out in the woods, do practice these things to ensure that you don't face any difficulty when you are forced to live out of your comfortable home.

Some essential tips: You should learn how to make simple shelters out in the wild like a debris hut.

Clothing & Personal Hygiene

The right body temperature isn't just maintained with the help of a shelter. You also need to wear the right protective clothes to keep yourself safeguarded against harsh weather elements, such as blizzards, rain, extreme cold and scorching hot temperature. Let us discuss what type of clothing items you need to stock for withstanding harsh hot and cold weathers, one by one.

Cold Weather

You must keep a separate bag for all the clothes to protect you against the chilly weather. Following the 'Layer Principle' created by the Special Forces Survival Guide, you need to layer yourself properly to insulate the cold air from reaching your body.

☐Body Wear

For that, you need to wear thermal underwear first followed by a wool shirt topped by a woven fiber sweater, or woolen sweater or a jacket and then wear a good quality jacket. The last layer needs to be both, waterproof and windproof. You must also have good quality headgear, such as woolen hats and air insulating caps, so you can prevent the 40 to 50 percent heat loss that takes place via your head with long earflaps. Make sure to stock at least five thermal under-wears, five wool shirts, five sweaters, three jackets and six headgears per person. You should also buy about five to six leg thermal per person and about six pairs of sturdy, water proof and long lasting pants/ jeans that are suitable for hiking in extremely harsh weather conditions.

☐Foot Wear

You must also invest in about two pairs of good quality waterproof boots per person to safeguard your feet against cold, water, snow, and heat. Choose boots that can help you hike and walk comfortably. Try selecting boots that are sturdy, but aren't too heavy since studies show that wearing even an extra pound on the feet can take energy from you that could have been used to carry objects weighing six pounds.

Additionally, you need at least ten pairs of good quality socks to keep your feet protected against harsh weather conditions. Choose socks that maintain a good blood flow in your feet, don't hold moisture, and are comfortable to wear, so you can maintain proper anatomical alignment that can help you hike easily and prevent premature fatigue in your feet and legs. Your socks must be able to maintain a moderate temperature in your feet, so you can hike easily in hot and cold weathers. You should also purchase about five to six liners per person. They are worn beneath the hiking socks and help wick all the moisture away, so your feet stay dry.

☐Hand Wear

You need to stock about six pairs of thin waterproof gloves and mittens each for each household member. First, you need to wear the thin gloves on your hand followed by the thick layer of mittens.

Warm Weather

For the warm weather, you must keep about ten pairs of lightweight and comfortable jeans per member, about 10 to 15 comfortable cotton tops/ shirts per person and about 10 cotton under-wears per person. Make sure not to use cotton tops in the cold weather as they have the tendency to hold water close to your skin, making your body temperature drop extremely low. You should keep about three flip-flops or sandals that you can wear in the extremely hot weather. Also, ensure that you keep loose fitted clothes, because tight fitted clothes can suffocate you in the hot weather.

How to Stock Clothes

Storing clothes the right way for your bug out bag is incredibly important. This is where you need to follow the COLDER principle created by the U.S. Air Forces. According to this rule, your clothes need to be:

C- Clean

O- Not overheated

L-Loose clothes in layers

D- Clothes must be dried

E- Examine clothes for any defects

R- Repair clothes when needed

Follow these guidelines and store your clothes properly and in the right amounts, so you and your loved ones can stay put and safe in any terrible condition.

Note:

Ensure to always have a second set of clothes, which you can remove once you get to your destination. The best way to stay warm is to ensure you are properly layered; if you want to cool down a bit, you can remove some clothes. You can also get some thermal shirts or pants. Here are a few ideas on what to have to stay warm:

☐ At least 2 T-shirts

☐ 2 long-sleeved button shirts- wear one and put the other in your bug out bag. If it is too hot, open the shirt or roll up the sleeves. The idea here is to stay warm irrespective of the weather.

☐ 1 extra size genuine thick wide plain leather belt- the backside can be used to sharpen a straight razor

☐4 pairs of cotton socks-you can wear 2 packs and pack the rest in the bug out bag. 2 pairs could be wool socks and the others cotton. If you want to wear 2 pairs at the same time, ensure to put on the cotton socks first then the wool socks. The idea is to ensure that your feet stay cold during hot weather and warm during cold weather.

☐2 pairs of long cotton underwear. Putting on long underwear can make the difference between survival and hyperthermia. You can put one on and the other in your bug out bag. To get extra warmth during cold weather, ensure to wear both pairs at a time.

☐2 lose fitting set of green, tan or brown jeans that are well suited for camouflage. Ensure to avoid wearing blue jeans since they often absorb water like a sponge and often suck lots of heat from the body especially when wet. You should ensure to wear 2 pairs of jeans at a time to protect yourself against cold weather.

☐A brimmed hat- this will help protect your face from the sun. You should also ensure to have mosquito hats since these can protect you from flying bugs, insects and gnats

You should ensure to have some of the following personal care items:

☐Ensure to pack some Q-tips to help keep your ears clean.

☐Tampons- although you can make your own by folding 2 or 3 thick cotton washcloths nicely then using one as you let the others dry after washing them.

☐Sharpening stone and straight razor

☐3 packs of dental floss, 3 good brushes and 3 large tubes of toothpaste (you will need to learn how to make your own toothpaste after some time).

☐Comb and/brush, 4 bars of antibacterial soap, 1 hand towel, 1 (16 ounce) bottle of shampoo, 1 pair of heavy duty nail clippers and a thick wash cloth

Note: Don't pack deodorants, colognes or perfumes since these often attract gnats and bees.

Once you've mastered how to stay warm (you have everything related to shelter and clothing), the next bit that you should learn as a prepper is how to prep for water because water is the next most important element after shelter (staying warm).

Chapter 3: How Important Is It To Be Prepared Mentally For A Disaster?

Some people are natural leaders and fighters. Survival comes naturally to them; they are athletic and think fast on their feet. While there are others who keep tripping on their feet even while they are standing on level ground. In a family, not every member is a survivor nor is every member is clumsy. However, in order to survive during a disaster the most important strength is not physical strength. Through it will come awfully handy during a situation, it is not the most important one. The most important strength is mental strength which comes with accepting the fact that we are facing a disaster and we must do everything to come out alive and in one piece.

Some people tend to panic when faced with a situation that seems unbelievable and this panic sends them into a body lock, making them unable to move at all. It is essential to be able to recognize which member of your family belongs to which category. It is ideal to arrange prep sessions to judge how which family member reacts and to hand them responsibilities and guidelines likewise. Although family members can get separated during disasters, a prep session allows everyone to understand what goes on during a disaster and what steps need to be taken to make sure you stay safe.

Preparation sessions allow people to mentally absorb what is going on beforehand because they have already planned for such an event. However, if one is put amidst a disaster, they may end up running around in circles not knowing what to do and not understanding what might happen if they do not move. Preparation has got a lot to do with preparing your mind for such situations so that you can think clearly and plan out your course of action. Otherwise, you might end up being led away and following others which might not be the best course of action if these same people have no disaster survival training. The best course of action is to decide and form your own course and lead your family to safety.

Chapter 4: Cutting Down The Weight

In this chapter we'll take a look at 5 ways in which you can reduce the amount of weight your bug out bag holds. Because the heavier your bugout bag is, the harder it is to carry around, you want to ensure that you not only scrutinize the items that are allowed to call your bag home, but also that you consider alternative options.

Use the land

The ability to use the land as a 'compartment of your bag' will greatly depend on the area in which you live. If your home is one that's surrounded by a great deal of trees and other ideal hideout spots, then taking advantage of a bush, here or there, will definitely come in handy where reducing weight and staying stocked is concerned. The first course of action will be to know where you're headed and to have one or two alternate routes in the event that your primary route moves its way up on the 'risky' radar.

Once you've carefully mapped out the way you'll be traveling on foot, do a walk through and look at locations that you can use to store a bottle of water, a can of food or other supplies that you'll need. It is, of course, important that you remember where you store these items.

In a SHTF scenario, where you're trying your hardest to get to your bugout location as quickly as possible, there will be no time to pull out a shovel and start digging through the ground, or to start playing hide and go seek with items that you stored. Also, you will need to choose a place that isn't obvious (to avoid others from gaining access to your supplies before you do).

Tying items like flashlights to trees along the route or hiding heavier items like batteries underneath rocks is a great way to reduce the weight of your bugout bag.

Not so much water

Yes, this is the last thing many expect to hear when preparing their bugout bag. After all, if there's anything that you need to ensure that you have, it's water. So, why on earth would this book suggest that you cut down on the amount of water you carry? Well, the fact is that water's heavy.

This isn't to say that you won't need to have water in your bugout bag. However, if there is the possibility for you to get water from sources nearby, like streams or lakes, for example, then this is an option that you will want to consider. By doing so, you'll be able to cut down the amount of water you carry, to about one bottle and refill as you go along. Water purification tablets and water filters will therefore serve as your substitute and are great options as they are indeed, significantly lighter than the approximated 8 lbs per gallon that water weighs.

Think multipurpose

Rather than having one item that only serves a single purpose, considering multipurpose tools for your bugout bag will cut down on its weight and the amount of space that you use. Prior to putting an item in your bag, think of the other purposes that it can serve and see what items can be eliminated as a result. An example of this would be packing a roll of duct tape and refraining from adding bandages to your bag. Duct tape will work well as securing a splint or holding cotton swabs in place over a cut. Additionally, duct tape can be used as a substitute for rope and so, rope (or the amount of rope) is another item you'll be able to do away with.

Another thing that needs to be considered in the line of multipurpose is purchasing tools that come equipped with a wide range of functions. Knives equipped with a compass, can opener and other features should, therefore, be high on your list. Avoid multi tools that come equipped with items you won't be able to take advantage of. A wine opener, for example, won't come in handy when you're on the run as there is little likelihood that you'll be popping open a bottle of wine to enjoy when you're heading to your next destination.

Hunger won't strike as often

If you have ever found yourself in a less than ideal situation, then you're most likely, already aware of the fact that hunger has a way of hiding itself when stress levels are high. So, though on a regular day, three meals may be your minimum, this won't be the case when you're on the go in a SHTF scenario. Instead, you'll be more consumed with getting to your bugout location than filling your stomach, and thus, you'll be eating a lot less. However, this doesn't mean that you won't want to eat at all. In order to stay focused and energized, you're going to need to give your stomach some digesting to do and curb the appetite that you know exists, but is adamant at suppressing itself.

Rather than packing heavy meals, stick to easy to prepare, lighter variations. Cereal bars are a great option as is bread, chips and nuts. If you live in an area that's got more fruit trees than regular trees, you're already on the lucky side of things as you'll be able to snack along the way and keep full without the need to keep your bugout bag full.

No batteries required

Before cashing in on that great deal you saw online, it's worth considering the advantages of straying away from battery operated items. Your bugout bag, your shoulders and your back will thank you for not adding extra weight from batteries. There are so many solar powered items available to replace battery powered items and thus, doing a bit of investigating (to see which ones are trustworthy) as well as shopping around (to get a good price and an item that is of the ideal weight) will prove to be beneficial.

Chapter 5: Water Purification/Filtration Supplies

Yet another rule in the survival world is this: All water is dirty. Meaning; any water you collect is not safe to drink. The commercially bottled water you have stored away is okay to drink without purifying, but any water you pull out of a crystal clear stream or take from your rain barrel is considered unsafe to drink.

You must always purify your water, no matter how fresh and clean it is. The human eye cannot see all of the harmful bacteria, protozoa and parasites that are lurking in the water. If you are collecting water from any outside source, you have to assume an animal has visited that watering hole before you. Animals have no problem defecating in the water they are drinking. Unfortunately, humans are not always careful either and their fecal matter manages to contaminate the water as well.

Fecal matter contains a whole list of nasty things you never want to ingest. Some parasites can be fatal. Never take the chance of drinking water that you have not cleaned. There are several options you can use to make your water safe to drink.

Before we get to how to purify your water, it is important to point out that purification and filtration are not one and the same. Purification kills the harmful organisms in your water. Filtration does a good job of removing most of the organisms, but it is not one hundred percent effective.

Ways to Purify Water

Household Bleach

This is a favorite simply because it is cheap and effective. However, storing bleach to clean your water isn't the best idea. Bleach begins to lose its effectiveness after about six months. It is rather inexpensive, so it doesn't hurt to buy a gallon of bleach every month or so to keep on your shelf. Rotate accordingly so you always have a fresh gallon on hand. Dropping eight drops into a gallon of water is all that is necessary to purify water. For water that is especially dirty or cloudy, you can add up to 16 drops. Let the water it for 30 minutes. It helps to circulate the water before drinking to help get rid of the chlorine smell.

Water Purification Tablets

These are quick and easy to use. Drop a couple tablets into a gallon or liter of water and wait 30 minutes. The tablets are made with chlorine, although you can buy iodine tablets. The tablets are easy to pack in your bug out bag and great when you are on the go. You will need to store several bottles. Each bottle typically contains 30 tablets. You will usually need four tablets to purify a gallon of water depending on the brand.

Boiling

This is another quick and easy way to purify water. Once the water has been heated and reached the boiling point, any organisms in the water will be killed. While some experts suggest boiling the water for 15 minutes, this isn't really necessary. Once the water has reached the boiling point, the organisms are killed. Boiling any longer is a waste of water as it will evaporate. Boil the water for a minute and no longer.

Iodine

Iodine is an option, but it isn't really one of the best. Iodine can be rather expensive and you need about twice as much as iodine as you would bleach. However, iodine will store for a year or more in the right conditions. Anybody who is allergic to seafood/shellfish should avoid iodine. Typically, a shellfish allergy will also mean an allergy to iodine.

Solar Purification

If you have no other option, you could use the sun to purify your water. You will need a clean plastic bottle. Hopefully you can find one that is BPA free. Fill the bottle with water and place it on the roof or somewhere that gets direct sunlight. Placing the bottle on a reflective surface, like your survival blanket, will help heat the water faster. Leave the bottle in the sun for at least eight hours. If it is cloudy, you can still use this method, but you will need to leave the water in the sun for at least two days.

Filtration of Water

Filtering water should never be your sole means of cleaning water that you have collected in the wild. However, if it is, you need to do your best to limit the amount of water you drink that has only been filtered. Ideally, you would want to purify your water and then filter it.

If you are going to use a filter, choose one that has the smallest pore size available.

You want a filter that claims to filter 99.99 percent of all organisms out of the water. Anything less and you are taking a significant risk.

If you have water in a rain barrel that you know with absolute certainty it hasn't had any kind of animal contact, running it through a filter is fine.

To help extend the life of your filter, pour the water through a cotton shirt or other piece of fabric. This will catch some of the bigger particles that are in the water that would ultimately get caught in the filter.

Filters are not everlasting. Pay attention to the packaging of the filter you buy and keep track of the amount of water you are running through it. Some filters will have a window that changes colors when it is no longer effective.

Chapter 6: Managing During An Emergency

By properly and efficiently stocking your survival pantry, you are now ready should a disaster strike. However, when the moment does arrive, proper management of supplies is just as important to maximize what you have for the longest period of time possible. Before hitting the emergency pantry, remember that you may also have other sources of food left at home.

First In, First Out

The major rule of thumb here is to consume the oldest food products or the ones that you have stored the longest, and then gradually consume your way into the new ones. This ensures minimal wastage due to expiration, and thus maximum use of supplies.

Start with Perishables

Taking into account the fact that electricity may run out at any moment during a calamity (if it hasn't run out yet), you will want to finish first the perishables from your refrigerator, as well as other perishables, such as bread and garden crops.

Ransack the Freezer

When power runs out, the freezer can still last longer than the refrigerator, given that its doors are left properly closed for as long as possible. Thus, items from the freezer are consumed next after perishables from the refrigerator. You can cook these food items indoors with a natural gas stove or the fireplace, or outdoors with a camp stove or charcoal grill.

Your Survival Pantry Comes Last

Finally, when all immediate supplies of food have run out, it's time to open your well-prepared survival pantry. Most of your food items should be easily consumable, but if you can easily cook them, then by no means do so. FEMA and the American Red Cross also suggest candle warmers, chafing dishes and fondue pots as substitute methods to heat your food. Open the lid and remove the label of canned goods before heating. Most importantly, make sure to always have a watchful eye when using fire and to kill out the flames completely afterwards.

Again, Making a List Comes in Handy

So many preppers underestimate the power keeping a list. Indeed, staying organized especially during tough times can get you farther. Keep a list of available food items in your refrigerator and freezer, and tape them on the doors so that you won't have to constantly open them and waste energy just to check inventory.

Properly listing down the food items in your pantry will help you keep track of supply count as it diminishes. This gives you an early heads up in case you'll have to ration your food in order to survive longer.

Chapter 7: Prepping For Free!

No joke, you can gather prepping resources for free or nearly free. The biggest free resource you can get is knowledge. The internet is full of blogs, forums and press about prepping and how to. In addition to this though, your most valuable prep item is yourself. Your skills are what will get you through any SHTF situation and many preppers are self-taught survivalists. Reading a book from the library on herbal medicines and local plants is entirely free. To maximize what you're getting out of it take notes in a binder or notebook (you could even buy that from the dollar store). Learning skills will be extremely valuable in the event of social collapse; many simple skills have been lost within the population thanks to modern technology and the lack of need. For example cooking, sewing, and mending are all things that will keep you going when you're unable to purchase new or get take out.

Speaking of take out, growing your own food is an ideal way towards self-sufficiency and doesn't cost much more than time. If you're purchasing fresh produce you're likely throwing away hundreds of seeds. Many varieties of food you buy in the store produce viable seeds that can be planted and grown in our own back yard. Squash is ideal for this as is melon, cucumber, and even tomatoes. Some more tropical things like avocados and lemons might need a bit more work, as well as being brought inside if you live in a region where winters are cold. You're already paying for the seeds when you buy the food; it's simply a matter of getting them out so you can actually grow them. The biggest mistake many people make is putting them into an airtight container, this encourages mold and will ruin them. Choose organic produce and then wash any excess fibers or fruit slime off using a sieve. Lay the seeds out onto a dry paper towel and allow to air dry for several days. If you plan on storing the seeds long term you can vacuum pack into an airtight sandwich bag and then put them in the freezer. Frozen seeds don't last forever and each plant will have its own shelf life so check first to maintain viability.

You may also be able to find local trade and swap groups. Bartering is one of the oldest forms of trade, chances are you have stuff lying around, or skills that someone else might want. Consider offering these in exchange for prep items or others teaching you skills. This is a great way to get what you need without spending any money. You can advertise on free sites and Facebook groups locally and see what's out there, in fact there are often prepping swap groups online that meet locally for exactly this purpose.

Most people have heard of Craigslist but fewer have heard of a similar site called Freecycle, it's just that recycled or second hand items for free. The site is dedicated to items that are entirely free; all you have to do it go get them. Some locations also have Facebook pages for free items and Craigslist too has a free item section. These pages do come with the same warning as thrift and yard sale items that you need to be careful of expiry dates and anything that might be broken and dangerous.

In addition to getting resources you can also work on organizing what you have, taking inventory and making lists are things you will wish you had done in advance. Make a list of important phone numbers – many people don't bother to remember phone numbers anymore since they have cell phones. Print recipes that you can make using your survival items and put them into a binder or write them out in a notebook. Creating a family emergency plan is also one of the most important things for prepping. If you don't have a plan how will your family know what to do? Write this plan down and store it with your emergency items, practice it or discuss it with your family so that they are informed and comfortable with their roles in it. This will be the time to decide if you are bugging in or out so that you can get your plan together.

Chapter 8: Water

Water is by far the biggest challenge for an urban prepper. Water is heavy and bulky and a complete space hog. Unfortunately, there is no getting around it. You have to have water to survive. You need to have enough on hand to sustain your family for a minimum of 3 days.

How much water is that?

Figure 1 gallon of water for each person per day. This is enough water for drinking and preparing a few meals. It isn't enough water to clean with. Either double the amount if you want everybody smelling fresh and clean or be prepared to deal with some body odor.

A family of four would need 4 gallons per day.

4 gallons for 3 days=12 gallons.

While it would be great if you could store enough water to last your family 30 days, which is approximately 120 gallons, it may not be feasible for an urban prepper. The goal is to do the best you can while preparing to haul water from somewhere nearby. If you have outdoor storage, put your water in it to save the space inside your home for your food. Water isn't quite as sensitive to things like ventilation or dampness. It does need to be kept out of direct sunlight and extreme heat, especially if it is stored in plastic containers. Heat causes the plastic to release chemicals into the water. Choose vessels that are BPA free for storing your water.

If you live near a body of water, you can certainly venture out and bring it back home. However, this may not be safe. You must assume you will have to get your water without anybody detecting you.

You do have some options when it comes to storing water.

*Bottled water is an option, but it can get spendy. A single water bottle contains about 17 ounces of water. You need 1 gallon of water per day, which is 128 ounces. Each person would need about 7 to 8 bottles of water every day. A case of water contains 24 bottles. Assume you need 1.5 cases of water per day for the family. Multiply that number by 3 days, 30 days or however long you plan on storing water for. You can save money and space by buying 5-gallon water containers. DO NOT use old milk jugs to store water. They are not meant for long-term storage and will end up making a huge mess in your home.

*Stackable water containers. These are handy little square plastic containers that are designed to neatly stack on top of one another to create a bit of a brick wall. Each container holds about 3 gallons of water and has a handle and a spout. You can purchase a frame to hold the containers more securely or build one yourself. You can put these water walls in the garage, in a closet or even against a wall in a bedroom.

*Your water heater holds about 50 gallons of water. If this is going to be your backup water supply, make sure you disconnect it from your main water supply as soon as the power goes out or there is some kind of event that could lead to your main water supply becoming contaminated. You don't want the water tank filling with contaminated water.

When you buy bottled water to store, you can assume it is safe to drink. However, if you are using water from your water heater or will be collecting water from a river, lake or stream, you ABSOLUTELY MUST PURIFY THE WATER. All water is considered dirty and unsafe to drink, no matter how clear and clean it works. You will need to keep a good supply of water purification tablets with your food storage. Each tablet purifies a gallon of water. Typically, a bottle holds 30 tablets.

You can also use a filter to clean your water, but a filter does not remove all the dangerous contaminants. Filtration makes the water look cleaner and may make it taste better, but it doesn't make it completely safe.

Boiling water is always an option, but you must have a way to heat the water to do that. In an urban prepping situation, it is dangerous to use cook stoves in the house. Do so with extreme caution. If you have a source of heat, you only need to bring the water to a boil. As soon as the first bubbles hit the surface, the water is purified. You don't need to boil it for a set amount of time.

If you have a backyard pool or a hot tub, you can use this water, but it must be boiled or purified first. Ideally, you will want to wait at least 3 days before you turn to your pool water. When there isn't any power, your pool chemicals and filter will no longer be working. It takes about 3 days for the chlorine in the water to evaporate.

If you live in the suburbs, you can look into setting up rain barrels. This is a great way to store about 50 gallons of water collected from the roof of your home. You will need to check your county regulations and any home covenants. As shocking as it may sound, there are some counties that have made collecting rainwater illegal. Rainwater in general is supposed to be safe to drink, but when it runs off the roof of your home and into the gutters, it will be contaminated and therefore needs purifying before drinking.

Chapter 9: Essential Prepper's Defense Supplies List

An important part of prepping is preparing for the worst, which means being ready to protect yourself, your family, and home from people with violent intentions.

Camouflage

Locks

Guns

Ammunition

Knives

Pepper spray

The first rule of self-defense is if you can avoid confrontation, you should do so. Camouflage is used primarily in hunting and for the military, but it can be used to hide from people as well, especially if you need to move through a dangerous area. It won't be especially useful if you're in an urban setting, but for wooded areas, prairies, and sandy environments, it can help hide you.

If you remain in your home or find another building to use as your base, you will need to fortify it against intruders. Buy deadbolt locks, the more holes the better. This makes it increasingly difficult for an intruder to get into your home.

Additionally, the difficult they'll experience getting in means that you will have more time to get prepared for action as well as to get your family in a safe place within your home. Use a separate lock for the room or building where you are keeping your supplies, even if it is inside your main home base. You want to make it as difficult as possible for anyone to get at your supplies; your supplies are your lifeline.

Locks are all fine and good, but people are persistent when their survival is at stake and you will likely need to personally confront aggressive intruders. The most obvious weapon of choice is a shotgun or a handgun.

Purchase enough guns for everyone in your family (or for as many people as you plan on arming) and stock up on the corresponding ammunition. Guns and ammunition will be a prime item for bartering, so consider buying guns and bullets for that purpose.

Store your bullets away from your guns, so in case someone does break into your supplies, they will find themselves without ammunition.

Knives are another good weapon to have on hand; they are easily portable, easily concealed, and have other purposes besides defense. They are also good to give to people who you don't want to carry guns, either because of carelessness or lack of trust. Knives come in essentially every size, so stock up anything from Swiss army blades to Samurai swords (providing you know how to use it, of course).

The last method of self-defense you should add to your prepper list is a can or ten of pepper spray. It is useful against both unarmed and armed intruders (if you can pull out the can fast enough), and even aggressive animals. Pepper spray is meant to distract an attacker so you can run, so it is best to not attempt to stay and fight after you have sprayed someone in the eyes.

Chapter 10: Security

Having the necessary security to protect yourself and your family should be a given as a prepper. Owning guns, bows, and ammunition is a must, but as important as owning a gun or a bow is becoming proficient with one.

Guns

Hopefully, you'll already own guns you've bought or inherited that will take up some of the categories on this list. If not, get ready for some gun shopping! Here are seven categories of guns that each prepper should have:

Bolt Action Rifle: A solid, bolt-action rifle with a scope will put lead down at a farther range than any other weapon on this list. This rifle will primarily be used for big game hunting, but it can also be used as an anti-personnel weapon if need be. Many years back, new and dependable bolt action rifles could only be purchased for around $1,000 with the scope included. But those days are long gone.

Marlin, Mossberg, Remington, Ruger, Savage, Tikka, Weatherby, Winchester and more now all make budget oriented, good quality rifles that come with a scope for $500 to $600. As far as calibers are concerned, go with either .308 Winchester/7.62x51mm NATO or .30-06 Springfield. Both will drop the vast majority of large game in North America, and are two of the most common rifle rounds in the country (remember that you want guns chambered in calibers that are plentiful and can be found easily).

Semi Automatic Rifle: Next after the bolt action rifle would be a lighter rifle in semi-automatic, chambered for .223 Rem/5.56x45mm NATO or 7.62x39mm. These are not true 'assault rifles' (contrary to what some people say) but are rather military-style semi-automatics. Prime examples are the AR-15 (the best selling rifle in the United States), the Ruger Mini-14/Mini-30, and the AK-47/AK-74.

In a grid down situation, you have to be prepared for the worst. Total chaos could ensue, there could be no law enforcement, and you and your family could be on your own. Arming yourself and learning to become proficient with a modern rifle that can send a lot of lead downrange if necessary against multiple assailants in a chaotic environment is a responsibility you must take to defend your family.

22 Rifle: That's right, a good .22 rifle in semi-automatic is a category of its own. The .22 could actually end up being the gun you use the most. It's an excellent homestead weapon, capable of dropping any small game and even deer if you make the right shot.

Because .22 ammo is so small, it can be bought in bulk and takes up far less space than other calibers. You can fit several hundred rounds of .22 in the same space you could fit a box of 20-50 rounds of pistol or rifle ammo. Since you can store so much of it, you can keep your target practice up with the .22, and due to its low recoil, it is by and large the best caliber to introduce new and younger shooters to.

As far as manufacturers are concerned, the best .22 semi-automatic would be a tossup between a Marlin 60 and a Ruger 10/22. Both are extremely popular and very proven designs with a number of aftermarket accessories. The primary difference between the two is that the

Marlin 60 is a tube-fed design, whereas the Ruger 10/22 accepts detachable magazines.

Full-Size Pistol: A full-size semi-automatic pistol will serve as your primary sidearm in a grid down scenario. As far as calibers go, limit yourself to 9mm, .40 S&W or .45 ACP, as these are by and large the most plentiful pistol calibers available. 1911's, the Beretta 92-series, Browning Hi-Power, Glock, Ruger SR-series, Sig Sauer, Smith & Wesson M&P, Springfield XD's, or the Walther P99/PPQ are all proven and reliable designs that you should give special consideration to.

Revolver: In addition to a full size pistol, it would be wise to also have a double action revolver chambered in .357 Magnum. Revolvers may lack the capacity and quick reload capabilities of a pistol, but they're still nice to have due to their natural reliability and increased accuracy with the longer barreled models. Plus, a revolver chambered for .357 will also accept .38 Specials, increasing its versatility considerably. Ruger, Taurus and Smith & Wesson are the three manufacturers that are the most recommended for revolvers.

Concealed Carry Handgun: This is the handgun that you would conceal carry on an everyday basis and will serve as a backup handgun in a grid down scenario. Since this is the weapon you'll be packing daily, it's totally up to you what you want to carry. If you prefer .38 snubnose revolvers, that's what you should carry. If you prefer a small .32, .380 or 9mm automatic, excellent. Or if you carry a full size handgun, that's fine too. Whatever you prefer is what you should go with.

Shotgun: Go with a pump-action shotgun chambered in either 12 or 20-gauge and that can fit two different barrels. Quality pump action shotguns are inherently more reliable than semi-autos, and 12 and 20-gauge are the two most popular shotgun rounds in the United States. When loaded with buckshot, a 12-gauge shotgun is easily the best home defense weapon you can buy, but a 20-gauge will get the job done and is better suited for shooters who don't like the recoil of the 12.

As far as barrels are concerned, look for shotguns where you can easily switch between an 18.5-inch barrel for home-defense and a longer 26 or 28-inch vented rib barrel that is suited for bird hunting and clay pigeons. Some shotgun kits come with both barrels already in the package. With this combination, you'll essentially have two shotguns in one. When it comes to specific brands and models, the Mossberg 500 or the Remington 870 are easily your two best options. Both are affordable, proven, popular and come with an unlimited number of aftermarket accessories and options.

Ammunition. You can buy all of the guns you want, but without magazines and ammunition, what good is a gun other than being a club? In fact, you would be wise to spend most of your security money or gun money on ammunition and magazines. Rather than buy two or three different AR-15s and customize them with all of the neat accessories on the market, buy one basic AR and spend the rest of your money on ammunition. This same rule holds true for all of your guns: don't spend money on upgrades, spend money on ammo.

There are a few convincing reasons why investing in ammo is more important than accessories and upgrades. For one thing, when the grid goes down, ammunition will be in short supply. The only ammo you'll be able to use is what you have in storage and what you can scavenge from bartering and other means. As a rule of thumb, have a minimum of 1,000 rounds per caliber stored away in your stockpile.

In addition to ammo, stockpile as many magazines as you can. You can never have enough magazines. Like ammo, they'll be in short supply in a survival/grid down situation and what you have is what you have. As another rule of thumb, plan on purchasing a minimum of six magazines per pistol and ten magazines per magazine-fed rifle. All that it takes for a magazine to be put out of action is for it to be damaged, for the springs to be worn out, or for you to lose it. If any of those situations pops up in a grid down scenario, you'll be more than happy you stockpiled all of those magazines when the time comes.

The other reason why you should invest more money in ammo is for practice. Your goal should be to become proficient with each one of the seven guns we've talked about above, and proficiency will only come with lots of practice. All in all, it will take around another 1,000 rounds on the shooting range for you to become truly proficient with your weapon. Through these 1,000 rounds of ammo, you'll become more accurate, disciplined, and skilled with the weapon.

Your storage ammunition and your practice ammunition put together, you can plan on buying a minimum of 2,000 rounds per caliber. Ammunition of nearly any kind isn't cheap, so to ensure that you reach that goal of 2,000 rounds, pick up a box or two of ammunition every time you visit a sporting goods store or a grocery store that sells ammo. You'll be surprised how fast your stockpile will grow.

Bows and Crossbows. Besides guns, another weapon that you should consider investing in is a bow and arrows or a crossbow and bolts. In the hands of a skilled shooter, a bow or crossbow can be just as deadly as a gun. The only negative downsides to owning one is they take time and skill to become proficient with, some would say more time than a firearm, and it can be cumbersome packing around arrows.

Nonetheless, the pros of owning a bow or crossbow make it worth owning one. You can reuse ammunition (a major plus) and they are silent. If you want to keep the noise down as you hunt for food, leave your rifle or shotgun at home and take your crossbow with you.

Improvised Weapons. Finally, there's always the last resort option of making your own weapons out of purely natural resources. You can make your own clubs by tying stones to the end of hard sticks; knives by sharpening rocks or picking up bones or shards of glass; and spears by sharpening or tying a knife to the ends of long, green wooden poles. Another way to make a spear is to split the end of a thick piece of wood to make three or four individual, sharpened points. This kind of spear serves an additional purpose as an adequate fishing tool.

Chapter 11: Bugging Out And Bug Out Bags

So we have covered why you may want or need to bug out. In order to do this you will need to carry your supplies and tools with you in an organized way. Realistically if you're planning on bugging in and only leaving when you absolutely have to, the likelihood that you will be leaving a rush is very high. So the best way to be ready for this is to have a bug out bag ready to go at a moment's notice.

You can even keep your bugout bag in your car so all you have to do is jump in and drive and you will have your supplies with you. This also means that if you're out and about when the disaster strikes, you will have everything you need to increase your chances of survival with you at all times.

Choosing a Bag

So first you will need to get yourself a bag to use for bugging out. A standard bag won't be big enough but hiking and camping backpacks work well. Tactical bags are the most functional due to their Molle system that allows you to attach various items and Molle compatible pouches to extend the capacity of the bag.

I personally use the Condor Venture (**US link – UK Link**). Which is absolutely fantastic and I would highly recommend it because of its great design and handy features. Its entire main section can be un-zipped right to be bottom of the bag and all of the way around making for easy packing and easy access to items in the bottom of the bag without unpacking it entirely.

This bag is also incredibly comfortable which is something you need to keep in mind. The Venture has a rigid back board with padding on top which is something you should look for. This means the bag always keeps its shape for maximum comfort and no objects inside the bag will ever poke you in the back.

Another thing you should consider, which the Venture has, is chest and waist straps that will help support the bag when walking long distances. The Venture has a removable waist strap which is very handy meaning you have the option of only using it when you need it, then when you don't it doesn't get in the way. This also means that you can use the waist strap as a separate utility belt and add Molle Pouches to it which is very handy.

No matter what bag you choose, you should go for something that is at least 30 liters as you will need to carry a lot with you. So, what should you keep in your bag to unsure you have the best chance of survival as possible?

Blades and Cutting Tools

A good quality multi-tool is something you should have with you due to its wide range of uses. It's worth paying for high quality as the cheaper tools are prone to breaking and bending. I personally have the Leatherman Wave (**US link – UK link**) because I believe it's one of the best, high-end multitool models out there. Incredible quality and very strong. I pretty much use my Leatherman on a daily basis so it's worth getting a good one. Obviously a multitool will have knives on it, but this shouldn't be your primary blade.

A good quality full tang knife should be high on your list of priorities as they have a range of applications and are probably one of the most useful bits of kit you will have at your disposal.

You should also be carrying a folding saw and a fold up entrenching tool. For my saw I went for the Bacho Laplander (**US link – UK link**) and can vouch for its quality and fantastic cutting ability. This is great for shelter building and fire wood cutting. It's very compact when it is folded away, so fits nicely into a bug out bag. Folding entrenching tools like the Draper or the SOG (**US link** – **UK link**) are very cheap and will come in handy with shelter building, fire pits and latrines.

Shelter

Keeping a tarpaulin in your bag will give you a quick and easy way of throwing up a shelter without having to make one. As long as you can tie some cord between two trees and pin or weigh the tarp down then you will have something to shelter you from the elements. A hammock works well under a suspended tarp to keep you off of the cold wet ground and is a popular choice for many survivalists. You can go for something very lightweight and simple like the Grand Trunk Ultralight (**US link – UK link**) or something a bit more advanced with a mosquito net like the Grand Trunk Skeeter Beeter Pro (**US link – UK link**).

Foil space blankets are great items that can save lives in cold conditions. They can also be used as a heat reflector for a fire, a small makeshift tarp, a ground sheet, a large signaling mirror and to keep you cool among other things. So they are a great item to have.

Sleeping bags will add to the carry weight of your bag considerably. So unless you live in a very cold area, I would go for a military issue wool blanket instead (**US link** – **UK link**). Wool blankets will keep you warm even when they are damp, are fire retardant and they are more compact and lightweight than a sleeping bag.

Cordage

You should also keep some paracord in your bag as cordage is useful for a whole range of things. If you haven't heard of Paracord, it's the same thing used in parachutes and is very strong. It's thinner and therefore lighter than standard rope. It also has seven thinner strands inside it that you can remove as use for more delicate work and for things such as fishing lines. The standard that most Preppers use is 550 Paracord (**US link – UK link**).

Fire Lighting

Another thing that you have to keep on you is fire lighting equipment. Fires are obviously essential for keeping warm, cooking and boiling drinking water. Fire's also have a range of other uses which I go into in more detail in my book dedicated to fire (**US link – UK link**).

It's best to keep a couple of lighters as they are the easiest and quickest way of getting a fire lit. However it's always best to carry a more long term method of fire lighting such as a ferro rod. If you have never heard of a ferro rod, they are basically a hard metallic cylinder that when scraped with the back of a knife or something similar, will give off very hot sparks that are enough to ignite most fine tinder. They will last for much longer than a lighter so they provide you with both a backup fire starting method and a long term solution.

Eating and Drinking

You will want to get a good quality solid steel canteen with no coating to keep in your bug out bag too. Klean Kanteen (**US link – UK link**) are a good choice. This will allow you to boil water to make it safe to drink in the canteen itself as you can place it straight on the fire. To go with this you will also want to get mess tins. A stainless steel mug is also very handy for drinking out of and brewing up natural teas. Finally, a set of stainless steel cutlery is very handy indeed.

It may not always be possible or practical to start a fire to boil water for drinking, so you should keep some water purification tablets in your bag for this eventuality.

Medical Supplies

Medicine and first aid is a big part of any bug out bag. You need to be able to disinfect and dress wounds effectively so that the risk of infection is as low as possible. An infected wound could turn nasty quickly and with no professional medical attention, could turn into a very serious problem.

So you will want to keep antiseptic fluid or wipes, sterile dressings, bandages and tape. You can just buy a standard first aid kit or you can make your own. If you buy a readymade kit and it doesn't have a mirror, you should add one. If you get a cut on your face or back for example, you need to have a mirror to effectively examine and treat it. You should also throw some pain killers in there in case you need them.

Lighting

Lighting is also important, so I would recommend getting a good quality tactical LED flashlight to keep in your bag. Having a portable, instant form of light is invaluable. It's a good idea to also have a backup wind up light to use if you run out of batteries for your main flashlight or to use when you don't need as much illumination.

Communication

You should keep a radio in your bag, preferably wind up, so that you can keep up to date with radio broadcasts that may affect you. I would also recommend having a few snares and a NATO fishing kit (**US link – UK link**) so that you can feed yourself more effectively in a bug out situation.

It's also a good idea to keep a couple of pairs of spare cotton socks and some spare underwear in your bag as sanitation will be a concern. Similarly you should keep a toothbrush and tooth paste. A travel towel will also be very handy. One other thing that can be easily overlooked is toilet roll. You don't want to have to wipe with a pine cone! You can get toilet paper tabs (**US link – UK link**) that are very compact and expand when wet saving you room in your bag.

Chapter 12: 77 Things You Need In Your Shtf Stockpile Now!

Basics Start with your SHTF Stockpile

You've addressed the majority of the inquiries above, adapted some great tips and traps, and even made a bug out pack for you and your family. In this area, we'll talk about setting up your stockpile. This incorporates your water, sustenance wash room, medicinal supplies, devices and weapons.

Here is a little rundown of a portion of the key things you'll have to keep your stockpile both secure and free of any issues.

1. Air conditioning Unit - At slightest while despite everything you have some power it is shrewd to have one of these things. Days can get terribly hot with no cooling. Appreciate it while regardless you can.

2. Resealable Airtight Containers – Everything you prepare ought to be put away so you can see what it is, and ought to likewise be stamped plainly with the substance, close date, and date it went into your stockpile. Water/air proof compartments keep your sustenance ensured by keeping out dampness and microscopic organisms. These are shoddy to buy so I propose stocking up on them.

3. Racking – Keep your sustenance off the ground and on racking at whatever point conceivable. I utilize overwhelming obligation racking in my setup and bunch of it. Make association much less demanding.

4. Sustenance Grade Buckets – Another extraordinary path for keeping nourishment sheltered and dry.

5. Cleaning Supplies – Moisture isn't your lone issue. You additionally need to stress over pieces and earth, which can prompt to bugs, irritations, and rodents pervading

your stockpile. Continuously keep your region clean. Creatures convey huge amounts of various maladies. The exact opposite thing you need in a SHTF circumstance is to become ill.

6. Security – Keep your stockpile a mystery so others can't get to it. Additionally, keep it bolted up as another layer assurance. Everybody in my family has a key and obviously knows the area of all the stockpile reserves.

Once you've gotten your SHTF stockpile setup arranged to all your particular inclinations it's an ideal opportunity to begin stockpiling every one of your things. A question I get asked a considerable measure is what amount should somebody really stockpile. The answer I give is straightforward! Prepare as much as your space you have dispensed permits you to.

You can never be excessively arranged. The more stockpiling and prepares you have prepared and close by the better. More prepares mean you'll have the capacity to make due for a more drawn out period before expecting to renew your stores. It will likewise give you more things you can utilize while bargaining.

Make sure to rotate your stockpile around the sustenance's and things you're family quiet and utilize. Try not to get just what you're advised to in the books. Make your preparing arrangement customized for your requirements. For instance, you'll need to have any meds you require, or on the off chance that you have pets you'll need to stockpile things they'll require.

Here are some planning nuts and bolts you'll need to add to your stockpile. Other than sustenance and water, these things will prove to be useful.

1. Dutch Oven/Portable Camping Stove – Great for cooking. Simply make certain to likewise convey a lot of additional canisters for fuel.

2. Bic Lighters/Candles/Stick Lighters – Great for both including light and beginning flames.

3. Multivitamins – A great supply of vitamins will fill in the gaps for any supplements you won't not get on your constrained eating routine.

4. Utensils, Paper Plates, Napkins, Disposable Cups/Paper Towels - With a constrained measure of water to use for cleaning these are great options and can be obtained inexpensively in mass.

5. Hand Mill – I adore entire grain. It can be put away for drawn out stretches of time and is brimming with supplements. In any case, it needs to be processed before being utilized so's the place having a hand process proves to be useful. I propose utilizing a manual one since you won't not have admittance to control.

6. Sacks - Having both littler junk packs and overwhelming obligation sacks will be extremely helpful for keeping your home

clean. I have an expansive stockpile of sacks in all sizes.

7. Seeds – Having a decent accumulation of seeds is basic for long haul survival. This will permit you to develop a wide range of various yields to sustain your family far into what's to come.

8. Can Opener – You'll be managing a considerable measure of canned nourishment so having a manual can opener close by is an easy decision. I recommend having different reinforcements on the off chance that at least one each breaks.

9. Aluminum Foil – Great for both keeping things crisp and utilizing to cook nourishment over a start shooting.

10. Dish Pans – Works extraordinary for cooking and utilizing as a washbasin to clean yourself as well as your garments.

77 Items You Need to Have In Your SHTF Stockpile Now!

No stockpile is ever great. Be that as it may, here are a cluster of things each genuine prepper ought to firmly consider adding to their present stockpile on the off chance that they don't as of now have them loaded. Distinctive families will have diverse necessities and diverse needs, however the vast majority of these things will be among the first to get gathered up when a SHTF circumstance strikes. Get arranged now, so you don't pass up a major opportunity later.

1. Bathroom tissue – This is a vital one for me. A few people wouldn't fret not having this, but rather it's one extravagance I'd lean toward not to live without.

2. Liquor – Not useful for drinking, it's likewise awesome for cooking and sterilizing your injuries.

3. Torment Medication – Reducing soreness, fevers, and general torment is a smart thought in the event that you need to remain sound and normal. I recommend

stocking up on these things as they'll take off the racks immediately when a fiasco strikes.

4. Cleanser – Staying clean, and keeping things sterilized is imperative. You would prefer not to fall sick in a SHTF situation in the event that you can keep away from it. I stockpile both fluid cleanser and bar cleanser.

5. Weapons – You have to ensure your family is secured. Having a few weapons will likewise prove to be useful for chasing for nourishment if fundamental.

6. Ammunition – Your firearms won't work without ammunition. Make sure to stock up!

7. Scissors – Much more helpful than a blade as a rule and convenient in case will make your own garments not far off.

8. Blanch – I have a major stockpile of this and it is an incredible disinfectant to have close by.

9. Building Materials – The more materials you have set aside the simpler you'll have the capacity to make repairs around your home. You'll additionally have the capacity to deal with new tasks that could make your life somewhat less demanding. I have a decent estimated gathering of timber, nuts, screws and fasteners.

10. Hatchet – Great for hacking kindling. You'll be happy you have a couple of these stockpiled.

11. Cutting edge Sharpener – You're edges are of little utilize if there dull.

12. Batteries – I keep a stockpile of all sizes possible.

13. Salt – Not just will it be utilized to add flavor to sustenance; it can be utilized to cure your meat.

14. Sugar and Honey – Two superb nourishment sources that can be put away for a practically inconclusive measure of time.

15. Moment Coffee – If you're an espresso consumer you'll be upbeat you supplied up on this. Moment espresso will last inconclusively.

16. Ladylike Products – Besides there principle utilizes, there likewise useful for dressing an injury.

17. Solidify Dried Food – Commonly called MREs. These are extraordinary in light of the fact that they keep going quite a while, and can be put away effortlessly until required.

18. Canning Supplies – You'll need to stock up on these as they'll be very helpful.

19. Preppers Library – Start assembling your accumulation of DIY aides and how-to aides now. You'll need books covering an extensive variety of points you may experience after a SHTF circumstance. There won't be an Internet to Google things on so you'll require reference directs close by.

20. Kindling – Have an extensive store of kindling cleaved and put away in a dry place.

21. Charcoal – If you're low on kindling you'll need some charcoal to cook your sustenance with.

22. Canned Food - A principle wellspring of nourishment other than your garden.

23 Water – Can't live without it!

24. Wheat, Rice, Beans, Flour – Some of your key staple sustenance's. Having a decent stockpile of these is a smart thought.

25. Planting Supplies and Tools – You'll require the best possible devices to effectively deal with your garden like scoops, rakes, scrapers and so forth.

26. Cooking Utensils and Tools - Will make cooking much less demanding.

27. Toothbrushes, Floss, Toothpaste and Mouthwash – It's vital to have great dental cleanliness. Tooth torment can make life

hopeless. I likewise keep a store of Ambesol.

28. Jerky – Great long last meat that you can make in a wide assortment of various flavors. Marvelous sustenance for stockpiling.

29. Drain – Condensed and powdered drain are both great things to stockpile.

30. Angling Supplies – Fishing is a keen approach to supplement your nourishment stores.

31. Lighters, Candles, Oil, Fuel, Fire Starters – Being ready to make fire is absolutely critical.

32. Spotlights, Lanterns, Torches, and Glow Sticks – You require approaches to move around oblivious.

33. Washroom Supplies – Having cleanser, towels, razors, Q-tips will make life more lovely. Great cleanliness can avoid sickness and microorganisms.

34. Pop, Gatorade and Kool-Aid – Any non-water kind of beverages. Everybody can utilize some assortment.

35. Chasing Apparel, Body Armor and Camouflage – You need to have the capacity to move around inconspicuous at whatever point conceivable, You likewise need some additional insurance in the event that ever assaulted.

36. Outdoors Gear – This will make voyaging simpler. Particularly amid chasing trips, or in case you're compelled to bug out.

37. Rope, Stakes, Spikes, Tarps, and Plastic Rolls – Everything you have to construct a brief safe house if necessary.

38. Clothespins, Lines and Hangers – Good to dry your garments in the wake of washing. It's critical to keep garments dry to counteract microorganisms and form development.

39. Wheelbarrows and Carts – Excellent for moving around heavier burdens.

40. Outside and Winter Clothing – You require garments for all periods of the years and for all circumstances.

41. Shoes and Work Boots – I have a stockpile of both. Your feet require appropriate security.

42. Gloves – Heavy obligation gloves will spare your hands when working extended periods outside.

43. Bug out Bags and Backpacks – These are vital for supply runs, chasing trips, climbing trips and pestering out.

44. Electrical Tape and Duct Tape – They have a huge amount of employments.

45. Cans – I have all sizes and shapes stockpiled.

46. Generators, Solar Panels, and Wind Turbines – If you can make control than you're as of now a stage in front of every

other person. Simply be watchful how you utilize it. It can make you an objective.

47. Bikes – Great for shorter treks. Simple to explore, and less expensive to load with gas.

48. Hand Pumps and Siphons – Great for getting water, gas, and oil out of various tanks.

49. Cutting apparatus - This is one device that will make life much simpler.

50. Devices – Having a decent supply of sledges, wrenches, screwdrivers, indecencies and so forth will make your errands around the house less demanding.

51. Emergency treatment Kit – You need to assemble a thorough medicinal unit.

52. Physician recommended Medication – If you're compelled to take any doctor prescribed medicine you'll need to have a supply close by if things ever turn out badly.

53. Recreations – You'll need to have some kind of diversion available for your down time. Books, magazine, prepackaged games, cards, and dice are all great things to have close by.

54. Compact Toilets – If you lose running water having one of these could prove to be useful. You can likewise get a fertilizing the soil latrine or assemble a toilet.

55. Propane Cylinders – This will among the primary things to go. You ought to stock up on propane.

56. Fire Extinguishers – Handy on the off chance that you inadvertently begin a fire. Without one, you can lose your home from one mischance.

57. Mosquito Coils and Repellent – You need to maintain a strategic distance from always getting eaten alive by bugs.

58. Rain Gear and Ponchos – Keeping dry is dependably a smart thought. Particularly in the colder months.

59. Snowmobile – If you live in a region with loads of snow one of these will be basic in the winter.

60. Individual Items – Having additional things you require available is a smart thought. For instance, on the off chance that you wear glasses have a couple of reinforcements put away. In the event that you wear dentures have another set made and a lot of denture glue.

61. Domesticated animals – If you anticipate raising creatures begin little now and begin figuring out how to raise and breed them.

62. Pet nourishment and Animal bolster – If you have pets or are raising domesticated animals you'll require supplies for them moreover.

63. Beds and Inflatable Mattresses - You'll need save bedding close by. You'll never know when you'll in the long run require it.

64. Window Insulation Kits – Keeping the warmth in your home is vital amid the winter months.

65. Mousetraps, Rat Poison and Ant Traps - You have to control any pervasions before they escape hand.

66. Bikes – For getting around your range rapidly and inexpensively.

67. Sewing Supplies and Fabric – You'll require these to patch and make garments.

68. Waste Cans – Good for junk and as additional capacity.

69. Composing Materials (Pens/Pencils) – Will give you different exercises to do in your downtime, furthermore useful for keeping your logs of provisions and undertakings that should be finished.

70. Diaries, Scrapbooks, Diaries and Calendars – So you can record your considerations, recall critical events, keep nourishment logs, and monitor time.

71. Coleman Mantles - Good for longer term lighting.

72. Hard Cheeses (Encased In Some Wax) – The wax keeps the cheddar from developing mold and microscopic organisms. Can keep going for a long time thusly.

73. Protein Bars and Protein Drink – Good sources of required supplements.

74. Dried Pasta – Another extraordinary nourishment to stock up on.

75. Dried Fruits, Raisins and Fruit Strips – My family cherishes these so we stock up on these pretty intensely.

76. Jams and Jellies – Another extraordinary expansion to the stockpile.

77. Humidifier - It will diminish a portion of the dampness in the room you have your stockpile situated in. Microscopic organisms start developing when dampness gathers in a little range.

30 Things to Stockpile with a High Barter Value

As you may expect, a portion of the things underneath will cover with the rundown of things above. However things on this rundown I keep a different stockpile of, exclusively for the utilization of bargaining with if necessary. I keep this stockpile far from my primary stockpile to keep it less demanding to see what I have available for exchange.

Recall that, you ought to never deal with any things that you and your family truly require. You will be unable to discover a thing again once it's gone.

1. Silver and Gold – Many individuals trust this will be the main outstanding type of genuine cash if a SHTF strikes. I attempt to store as much as I mindfully can.

2. Cigarettes – I don't smoke myself, however individuals who require their nicotine will exchange practically anything to get it. That makes this a profitable item.

3. Liquor – Another regular need that individuals would prefer not to do without.

4. Batteries – If you need to control a littler handheld thing you're going to most likely need a few batteries. That makes these extremely profitable.

5. Ice-If you make sense of an approach to store and make ice you'll be in a fabulous trading position.

6. Control - Items like sun based power packs will be exceptionally alluring once the network goes down.

7. Canning Lids – Most individuals disregard this one making it important on the off chance that you have a stockpile of them. They are a basic piece of protecting sustenance.

8. Water Filters – Clean water measures up to survival. Having channels will make life much less demanding.

9. Seeds - People should develop nourishment. Keeping in mind the end goal to do that they will require seeds. This makes them incredible for bargaining.

10. Medication – People will dependably fall sick. Drug will get a genuine premium in a SHTF circumstance.

11. Candles – People need to live in the light not the dull. Candles permit them to illuminate their nights with next to no bother.

12. Ammunition – You can simply utilize some more slugs for your weapons.

13. Tissue – Not something I'll exchange away, which makes it all the more profitable to individuals who are similarly invested.

14. Outdoors Supplies - People will persistently require dozing packs, tents and other outdoors outfit.

15. Cleanser – Clean garments is an extravagance many individuals would prefer not to live without.

16. Battery Operated Radio – This will be a looked for after thing for individuals hoping to get overhauls after a debacle strikes. Individuals need to comprehend what's going on.

17. Sugar, Salt and Honey – Three staples nobody needs to do without.

18. Weapons – People will need to protect themselves. These can get a high premium.

19. Water – If you have additional that you're willing to part with, individuals will pay for not finding it and channel it themselves.

20. Canned Food – People will dependably hope to add to their nourishment stockpiles.

21. Information and Skills – If you were a jack of all trades you can exchange those

aptitudes in return for something you require. Will work with a wide range of things.

22. Fuel – People will dependably require more fuel to run their vehicles and generators.

23. Pot – People who have restorative conditions will pay an incredible arrangement to motivate something to assuage their side effects. Not my thing but rather a feasible dealing thing in a SHTF circumstance.

24. Drain and Cheese - If you have a decent wellspring of crisp drain and cheddar you'll get a premium for it.

25. Building Supplies - People will dependably need to do repairs and work on new tasks. In the event that you have additional provisions like screws, nails and wood you'll be in a decent position.

26. Vegetables – If you have a garden you can exchange for heaps of products with your additional harvests.

27. Apparatuses – Having additional saws, sledges and hatchet's to exchange with will bring you a decent cost in kind.

28. Diversion – Items like books, tabletop games and toys will be a well known thing to exchange particularly among individuals with youngsters.

29. Apparel1 and Sewing Supplies – If you can make your own garments you can pivot and bargain for things you're running low on.

30. Meat – If you breed your own domesticated animals and have an excess of meat you'll be a prevalent individual to exchange with.

Chapter 13: Tips And Tricks For Surviving A Natural Disaster

One of the biggest threats that a prepper has to prepare for is a natural disaster. Natural disasters take the form of many things, including hurricanes, tornadoes, earthquakes, floods, and so on. The scary part about natural disasters is that they can occur literally anywhere. Even if you don't live on the coast where you could be affected by a hurricane, you may live more inland and be affected by a tornado or a flash flood, for instance.

The other scary aspect of natural disasters is that they are entirely outside of our control. If you think about it, we really live our daily lives at the mercy of mother nature. For this reason, you may think that the only thing you can do when disaster hits is turn, run, and hope you're spared.

But this is not true. By having the right skills and gear on hand, your chances of surviving the next natural disaster to come your way go up dramatically. In this article, we will cover ten tips and tricks that if you apply successfully will dramatically boost your chances of making it out alive when disaster hits.

·Organize Yourself

-This one is huge and yet so commonly overlooked by many preppers. You can't just be prepared, you have to be organized in how you prepare. This means coming up with different emergency plans for different scenarios, having all of your gear be organized instead of crammed all into one spot, and so on.

·Designate a Rendezvous Point

-You must be prepared for the possibility that disaster strikes while your family members are separated from one another. Come up with different escape routes from your home and other areas where your family members may be, such as at work, at school, or so on, that all lead to one rendezvous point or meeting area that you know to go to when the disaster hits.

·Have Emergency Contacts

-Emergency contacts are friends or family members you call outside of your local area but within driving distance of you. This way, they can more effectively lend you aid and even offer you a place to stay for the time being. It may be that the home of an emergency contact is your rendezvous point. Every family member in your home needs to be aware of the emergency contact(s) and all contact information for them.

·Have a Weather Radio

-It is extremely important that you have a weather radio with you so that you can not only be kept up-to-date as the disaster is actually happening but possibly even be warned of the disaster before it hits. This way, you can make a decision as to whether you should bug out or not, and you can round up your family and get out of dodge before the disaster hits and the roads become jammed with traffic.

·Have a Working Bug Out Vehicle

-Your bug out vehicle (BOV) needs to be an AWD or 4WD vehicle with seats for at least four people and enough gear to haul all of your supplies. What's more, is your BOV needs to be ready to go so you can evacuate as soon as possible. This means it must be properly maintained and have plenty of gas cans on standby (the gas stations will be jam packed with people). Your BOV can either be an additional vehicle you have or it can be the car you drive every day, but ideally it should meet those qualities we set.

·Have an Axe and Life Vests Stashed in Your Home

-The life vests are meant mainly for flooding situations, but the axe will be arguably even more helpful. If you're trapped in your house while the water levels are rising, you can use an axe to break down the doors and escape. Or, if there's a tornado and you need to get inside somewhere fast but it's locked, you can use an axe to break through as well.

·Fill Up Your Bathtub the Moment the Disaster Hits

-Water is absolutely critical in any survival or disaster scenario, but something that many preppers don't think about is how sanitation standards going to drop considerably when disaster strikes and likely stay that way for many weeks. This means clean water is simply not going to be easy to find. By filling up your bathtub, you'll provide yourself with an immediate source of clean water.

·Practice Your Skills (A Lot)

-Last but not least, you should certainly practice the above skills if you want any hope of things going according to plan in the chaos of the disaster. For example, you can't just come up with an evacuation route to a rendezvous point, you actually have to practice driving to that rendezvous point so that you have it memorized and can come up with alternate routes in the process. Run drills with your family on a periodic basic so you can make sure that everyone not only knows what to do when disaster hits, but that they are capable of doing it as well.

Chapter 14: Kits

Assemble a Bug Out Bag

A bug out bag is a bag of equipment that should enable you to survive at least 72 hours (3 days). As a prepper you should always have your BOB sorted however, if you are new to prepping you need to create your BOB now. Your kit could be the difference between life and death.

Everyone has different items in their BOB according to their skills however the following should be a good starting point.

Backpack (I am sure this needs no explanation)

LED Flashlight (with spare batteries)

Survival knife with sheaf

Water and water bottle

Means of purifying water (tablets, life straw, etc)

Waterproof matches

Pencil Sharpener – Can be used to sharpen sticks for arrows as well as creating tinder

Fire striker

Candle

Shelter (tent, tarp, etc)

550 paracord

Sleeping bag

Stove and fuel

Duct tape

Food and energy bars

Sewing kit

Soap

Wind up radio

Multi-tool

First aid kit

Money

ID and emergency contact numbers

Map and compass

Bandanna

Simple fishing kit

Hygiene necessities

Tin opener

Spare set of clothes

You may find you choose to replace items from the list with other items however the above is a good starting point. I personally use extra items not on the list but that is just down to personal preference and skills.

Perform regular test runs. Go spend a few days in the wilderness and you will soon see if you have too much or too little. Is there something you could have done without and used your surroundings instead? Is there something you really needed but didn't have? By doing test runs you can find out early which is much better than finding out once it is too late.

Believe it or not, there is both a correct and an incorrect way of packing your bug out bag. Too much weight at the top and you run the risk of being knocked off balance. Too much weight at the bottom causes you to have to lean forward to balance that weight on your hips which could result in damaging your back.

Divide the Weight

The first step in correctly packing your Bug Out Bag is to separate all the items by their weight. You should create three piles, one for the heavy items, one for the mid-weight items and finally, one for the light items. Doing this will be of great help when it comes to putting everything in the BOB.

Now, depending on the type of pack you have will depend on where you place the heavier items. If you use an external frame pack then you need to place the heavier items up towards the shoulders whereas if you use a pack without a frame, you need to place the heavier items near your hips and close to your spine.

How to Pack

Heavy Items – You need to place the heaviest items in the middle of your bug out bag. Items that can be broken down, should be. A tent has not just the tent, but also poles, pegs, etc so these can be placed elsewhere to help cut down on some of the heavy items.

Mid-Weight – These are not heavy and can be placed around the pack to evenly distribute the weight. Remember what we said before about keeping the weight towards your spine.

Light Items – Finally we have the light items which can be placed in the side pockets as well as the top of the bug out bag. To save you having to keep rooting through your bug out bag, place the most used items in the side pockets such as your navigation tools, fire lighting equipment and snacks.

Adjustments

Once you have all of the above sorted, it is time to make sure your pack is correctly adjusted for your body. Your pack may have quite a few straps but each has it's own use so adjust them until they are perfect.

Hip Belt – Pick up your pack and get it on your back. Pull the hip belt around your body and clip it up. Tighten the straps evenly. You need to try and keep a margin of around 1 inch on both sides. Your hips should hold around 80 – 90% of the pack's weight.

Shoulder Straps – Pull back and down on the straps to tighten them so that they are close to your body and wrap around your shoulders. These straps are not intended to hold any weight, they are to simply hold the pack against your body.

Load Lifters – You can find the load lifters located just above the collarbone and attach the top of the pack to the shoulder straps. Gently pull them to take some weight off of the shoulders.

Sternum Strap – This is located at the chest and is used to prevent the shoulder straps from slipping off. Adjust to a comfortable height across your chest that pulls the shoulder straps in.

Stabilizer Straps – Not all packs will have stabilizer straps but if so, they can be found near the hip belt at the bottom. Evenly pull them in to your body to secure and stabilize the load.

Assemble a First Aid Kit

Having your cupboards full of food and water is all good but what happens in a SHTF scenario when you do not have the supplies to deal with your own wounds? They could become infected and then you might be in a whole host of trouble. If you are planning on sticking around in an urban environment than your urban first aid kit is essential.

Below we are going to cover the bare minimum that you should be putting in to your urban first aid kit.

10 x Alcohol swabs

Antibiotic cream

4 x Burn gel packets

40 x Assorted band aids

6 x Blister patches

Waterproof tape

10 x Small gauze pads

6 x Large gauze pads

2 x Gauze rolls

Ace Bandage

SAM splint

Paracetamol

Ibuprofen

Aspirin

Antacid Tablets

8 x Butterfly Strips

Razor blade

Non-Latex gloves

Quikclot wound dressing

Scissors

Eye wash

Thermometer

Large needle

Matches/lighters

Tweezers

Emergency blanket

Flashlight with spare batteries

Kit For Your Vehicle

The whole idea of being a prepper is to "prepare". This goes for your vehicle too. If you take off in your vehicle and something happens, there is only you to blame for not having what you need around you. Now hopefully you will never have to use it, but not one of us knows when something will happen. Don't put it off, create your emergency car kit now.

When it comes to what you choose to include, it will depend on factors such as age, medical conditions, etc, however the below is a starting point for those who have yet to create their emergency car kit.

Tire iron, jack, spare tire

Emergency contact information – If something happens to you, responders need to know who to call. If your phone goes down, you will also need numbers. Only keep this information in the car whilst driving.

Flashlight – Some people choose to also have a spare but I just keep the one with spare batteries.

Extra clothing – This includes a pair of good gloves as these are great when it comes to working on your vehicle.

Water – Helps to stop you becoming dehydrated but will also help to keep the radiator cool.

Empty gas can – not all stations sell these so it is a good idea to carry an empty one in the car.

Tools – spanners, socket set, screwdrivers, pliers, etc

Duct Tape – has a million uses

Multi-tool

Jumper Cables and/or jump box

First aid kit

Blanket

Candle

Protein bars

Lighter

550 Paracord

When it comes to storing food in your vehicle it is better to go for dry foods as they will not be affected with the changes in temperatures.

Don't Forget the Sewing Kit

A basic sewing kit is often a forgotten item by preppers. Being able to clothe and keep your family warm is very important following a crisis and being able to sew is just as important. You need to be able to repair your family's clothes.

Simply adding a sewing kit in to your emergency supplies is not enough, you need to actually know some basic sewing skills. The good news is that sewing is not actually a hard skill to learn, ask around family members as I am sure some will have at least a basic understanding.

Another good reason to learn sewing is that it can also be used as a bartering skill after the SHTF as it is a skill that few understand anymore. An easy start would be to learn how to sew a button back on an item of clothing and how to repair a hole. It is easy going once you get them down.

So you have two choices for your sewing kit. You can either purchase a basic sewing kit, or you can put your own kit together which we are going to look at below.

In order to put a kit together you are first going to have to get yourself some kind of container that will contain your sewing kit. This can literally be anything that you like and any size that you need. What IS important is the items that you add to the kit. I recommend the following items though you can add extra items if you feel it is needed.

Scissors

Sewing Needles – Selection of sizes

Pins

Safety Pins

Measuring Tape

Seam Ripper

Buttons – Selection of sizes

Thread

The above items should always be added to any basic sewing kit though other items can be added such as thimbles and threaders if you feel it is necessary.

Chapter 15: Communication

When the grid goes down most, if not all, of the ways that we've become accustomed to communicating with people will be gone. We won't be able to reach people via messaging on social media, by texting or calling by phone, or by e-mailing. Therefore, you'll need new ways to contact people and to hear about what's happening in the outside world when the grid goes down. The good news is that you won't have to resort to fire signaling to do so.

Satellite Phones. Every prepper should have a pair of satellite phones somewhere in storage, with at least one preferably in their bug out bag. Satellite phones are expensive, both for the actual phone and for service. If it's going to put a dent in your wallet to acquire and use a satellite phone, don't buy one. But if you are in a financial position where you can afford one, there is no excuse not to get one.

In the event that satellites are still up and running in a grid down scenario or a natural disaster, satellite phones will be your best way to contact people. Yes, that is one limitation for them right there that you've noticed: they need satellites to work. But as long as there are satellites up and running, satellite phones will provide you with a reliable means to call other individuals.

CB Radio. It's surprising that CB radios are the most popular communication device preppers stockpile, because they are quite limited in their range. This is because the power output in CB radios is weaker than other communication devices, so they can't transmit a voice message as far as your other options. But remember, you can't put all of your hope in just one communication device. Diversify and buy a number of different communication devices. CB radios are cheap, and for that reason they are a quick and easy purchase for many preppers. Don't bet your life on getting word out with a CB radio when the grid goes down, but it won't hurt your survival chances at all to put one in your stockpile.

HAM Radio. The most reliable communication device you could buy? Without a doubt, it's the HAM radio. HAM radios have been used for years by preppers, law enforcement and search-and-rescue teams alike. Adding to their appeal is their ability to pick up weather forecasts. This means you can plan out your day well in advance based on what the upcoming weather entails.

HAM radios are also more powerful than the other options and can transmit a message farther than nearly any other affordable communication device. Are HAM radios the only survival communication device that you should buy? Absolutely not, as you should buy as many different communication devices as possible. In a real survival or grid down scenario, however, you may end up using the HAM radio more than any other of your communication devices.

Chapter 16: First Aid

Last but certainly not least, we come to something you hopefully never have to use but that you may have to; first aid. It can be a scary thought to be injured and in need of first aid, but becoming hurt is a real possibility and one you must be prepared for. In that regard, having a custom, well-stocked medical kit is something you absolutely must have.

When putting together your medical kit, you have to do more than simply buy a cheap first aid kit at a sporting goods or grocery store and consider yourself well stocked when it comes to first aid. It's more than just having a first aid kit; you need to be completely familiar with its contents and know how to use them. Cheap first aid kits at the store will have some of what you need, but it's likely going to be cheap quality. Besides, are you really going to pull apart that first aid kit when you get home and dissect its contents? Probably not.

This is why you should buy all of the components for your first aid kit individually. This will be slightly more expensive, but in the long run, you'll be completely familiar with everything in your kit. Give consideration to putting together more than just one custom first aid kit; remember the old adage to never put all of your eggs in a single basket.

Keeping a medical kit in your bug out bag, in your vehicles, in your garage, in your home, and wherever else you keep your survival supplies is something a wise prepper would do. What happens if you keep your only medical kit in your bug out bag but you get injured while out on the road and your medical kit is back home?

Here is a checklist of the absolute minimum supplies every custom medical kit needs. Just like the checklist for the bug out bag, you can add items to this list as you see fit, but this is what every custom kit will need at the absolute least:

-Antibiotic Ointment

-Aspirin

-Bandages (assorted sizes)

-Bandana

-Blankets (wool and space blanket)

-Chap Stick

-Cloth

-Cough Drops

-Cotton Balls and Cotton Swabs

-Duct Tape

-First Aid Manual

-Flashlight (small)

-Gauze Pads

-Gel (Aloe Vera)

-Glow Sticks (avoid red)

-Hand Sanitizer

-Ibuprofen

-Knife

-Needles and Thread

-Pain Relievers

-Pens and Paper

-Prescription Medications

-Matches

-Medical Cup or Bowl

-Mirror

-Scissors

-Spoon

-Sunscreen

-Syringe (at least 2)

-Tape (adhesive)

-Thermometer

-Tweezers

-Tylenol

-Vaseline

You should become very familiar with all of these items and know what situations they will be needed for. You should consider taking a survival medical course to gain the knowledge and experience to use these items. You don't have to know how to perform a surgery out on the field, but you should know how to treat simple injuries. To treat those injuries, you need to be familiar with all of the contents inside of your kit, and the best way to be familiar with those contents is to put together a custom medical kit.

Since accidents can happen in a survival or grid down scenario, it's also important that you have knowledge on how to treat serious injuries with the minimal resources available to you in addition to having everything you need in your survival kit.

Treating Fractures and Broken Bones. If you or a member of your group suffers a broken bone while stranded in the wilderness or in a grid down scenario, it has to be treated as soon as possible. A broken bone can be treated even if you lack the medical equipment you would find in a hospital

There are two kinds of broken bones that can occur in the wilderness: open fractures and closed fractures. In an open fracture, the broken bone will stick out of the flesh and skin. In this case, you have two immediate problems on your hands: a broken bone and a bloody open wound. In a closed fracture, the bone will be broken but will not stick out to create a flesh wound.

Symptoms of a broken bone will include the possible sound of the bone snapping, a lot of pain in that area, discoloration and/or swelling of the skin, and a loss of mobility in that affected area. If left untreated, a broken bone can lead to numbness, internal or external bleeding, and shock. For those reasons, a broken bone is best handled when it is treated as soon as possible.

To treat the broken bone, you'll need to find two, thick branches or sticks that are as long as the limb. Wrap cloth or other padding around the branches if those resources are available. These two branches will make up the splint. This splint should be tied around the limb on both sides with whatever you have. Clothing, rope, string, or vines will all work well. The splint should be secured in three areas: around the ankle/wrist, the knee/elbow, and just below the hip/shoulder.

Elevate the affected area to increase blood circulation, stay hydrated, and take plenty of rests. A headache will set in eventually, so to minimalize it, take Tylenol or ibuprofen tablets and wrap a damp bandana or piece of clothing around your head. Eat plenty of food to stay energized.

If the broken bone is an open fracture, stop the bleeding by tightly wrapping a bandana or rope above the wound, and then use gauze pads or bandages to seal it off. Avoiding getting debris or dirt in the open wound.

Treating Dislocations. A dislocation differs from a broken bone or fracture in that a limb is forced out of alignment rather than being broken or snapped. Dislocations can be more painful than fractures and are just as lethal; if the dislocation remains untreated, it will inhibit blood circulation and cause nerve damage. Symptoms of a dislocation include pain, swelling and skin discoloration in the affected area, a likely malformation of the affected joint, and limited movement.

Since dislocations are immensely painful, take a pain reliever before treatment. For the next step, the process will go much smoother if someone else is present to help treat you. The dislocated bone will need to be pulled from the joint. Yes, this will be very painful on top of the pain you or your group member already feels from sustaining the dislocation, and will probably require multiple tries.

As the bone is pulled away from the joint, this will put space in between it and the joint. The bone should be pushed back into the joint slowly but firmly. The human body is designed a certain way, so because of that, it's physically natural for the bone to want to be placed back into the joint. While the process of actually slipping the bone into the joint will be incredibly excruciating, the reward will be very gratifying: much of your mobility will be restored, and much of the pain will immediately go away.

The affected joint will still be sore and range of motion will be temporarily limited. To continue to treat the joint, create padded splints and then recreate the process you would have used for treating a broken bone. The splint should remain in place for at least a couple of weeks minimum.

Treating Sprains. Sprains may not be as serious of an injury as a broken bone or a dislocation, but the longer it is left unattended, the more serious the injury will become. A sprain is simply where a ligament or tendon becomes overstretched, leading to symptoms of swelling, tenderness, skin discoloration and pain in the affected area.

Once you or a member of a group is believed to have suffered a sprain, lay down and rest the sprain immediately. You should not move for the next twenty four hours. Soak a piece of clothing or bandana in cool water and place it around the sprain. The injured area should be left stabilized and elevated to ensure healthy blood circulation.

Following the initial twenty four hour time period, create a small splint to keep the area steady. This splint will need to be kept in place for a week at the least and two weeks at the most. Following the treatment process, the affected area may remain sore for a few more days, but mobility will be restored.

Chapter 17: A Quick Guide to Urban Prepping

A Quick Guide to Urban Prepping

Attempting to survive a long term SHTF circumstance will require a ton of prepping, training and diligent work. Be that as it may, in the event that you live in a urban region with many individuals per square mile than you have to set yourself up a little uniquely in contrast to somebody who lives out in suburbia or a more remote area.

The purposes behind this are you'll in all probability have less space to store your prepping and to make ventures for use down the line. Likewise, once a debacle occurs you'll no doubt need to bug out.

I wouldn't propose attempting to make it long haul in a city domain. You won't have space, security, or the capacity to grow a bigger garden. You'll additionally think that it's hard to discover access to clean water, and you won't have the capacity to chase for your own sustenance.

Tip #1 - Know every one of the courses out of the city you live in. Once SHTF, individuals will frenzy, and it will get harsh out there genuine snappy. It's a smart thought to have your bug out sack prepared, a bug out area scouted out, and information of each reasonable course out of the city. A decent approach to get out speedy is by utilizing any old deserted railways, and tailing them away.

Tip #2 - Once a power outage or power blackout happens, start assembling all the water you can. Since you won't have simple access to water it's imperative to accumulate as much as you can before every other person sticks to this same pattern and does likewise. On the off chance that you've chosen to bug in, make certain to top off your bath, sinks, containers, basins and whatever else you can with water.

Tip #3 – Don't take part in battling others. Individuals will begin to freeze and get brutal searching for provisions once a debacle happens. Try not to get drawn into anything unless totally vital. You may deteriorate which will enormously diminish you and your friends and family capacity to survive long haul.

Tip #4 – Get inventive when searching for nourishment. In case you're in the city and need to chase for nourishment bear in mind to check candy machines, shut down rec centers, an office working with cafeterias, and close down eateries.

Tip #5 – Don't give your weapons or walkie-talkies a chance to show when out in the open. Individuals will need to take your prepares and weapons; Showing that you have these things will make you an objective.

Tip #6 – Have an ordinary convey unit (EDC) on you. This is a basic unit, which will bail you out in a urban fiasco occasion.

It comprises of a Bic lighter, jug of water, collapsing blade, some additional money, multi-device and a compact radio. You can fit these all pleasantly in a little tablet pack.

Tip #7 – Go sun oriented. Notwithstanding when you live in a littler condo you can do a great deal of things to diminish your need of force drawn from the network.

Tip #8 – When bothering out you might need to discard your auto or whatever other type of open transportation. Chances are the city will get totally gridlocked before you can get out securely. This could abandon you encompassed by individuals hoping to plunder or uproar. You need to maintain a strategic distance from individuals as much as you can while bothering put.

Tip #9 – Don't attract thoughtfulness regarding yourself. Try not to wear disguise or give any sign that you've arranged for a debacle. This will make you an objective. Pants and a shirt will work fine and dandy. You need to mix in, not emerge.

Tip #10 – If you're bothering in don't go close to your windows. You don't need anybody to know you're area. This is a wellbeing measure I recommend taking after. Getting seen may make you and your home an objective.

Tip #11 – Have some ecological catastrophe outfit put away in your bug out packs. This incorporates eye security, respiratory/lung assurance, listening to insurance and hand security.

As should be obvious there is a great deal of things to consider when urban preparing. This is only the tip of the ice sheet. On the off chance that you anticipate irritating in while living in a urban domain I recommend accomplishing more research and making your home as productive and arranged as could be expected under the circumstances for a long haul SHTF circumstance.

Chapter 18: Shelter Items Need To Be In Your Bug Out Bag

You cannot stay outside in the elements. You must be able get away from the wind, cold, heat, and any other pests, bugs, and other nuisances. You must be able keep dry.

Exposed to the elements is one of the leading causes of death. Hypothermia is a condition where the body is too cold to function properly. It can happen in minutes or gradually creep up on you, without you realising. Hypothermia can be described as "an unintentional decrease in the body temperature".

Your core temperature should not drop below 35 degrees. Advanced hypothermia or unconsciousness can occur below 28 degrees. It is possible to feel the air temperature drop below freezing without shelter. This is especially true in winter.

Without shelter, you can be more susceptible to infection, serious injury, and even death.

You can make shelter with lightweight and portable items. It is important to have something with you when creating shelter. A tarp (tarpaulin) is one of the most convenient options. Even though it is not a tent, it can be used to provide shelter from wind and rain as well as a safe sleeping area.

It is lightweight and small, making it a great choice for survival and bushcraft enthusiasts who are familiar with how to make a shelter. Although this shelter is versatile, it's best suited to one individual.

You can always take a tent with you and bring a tent for one or more people. This has obvious benefits, such as the ability to have a shelter that is ready to go. However, it can also lead to an increase in weight and bulk. This could mean that you may have to leave behind some equipment.

Multi-family tents are a great addition to your bug out bag. To be completely honest, I wouldn't go that route. Keep things simple.

You may be able to shelter yourself en route and not need your own bag. Keep in mind, however, that the tent is heavier to transport in your bug out bag the more people that will use it.

Additional items for the Bug Out bag

You will need other things than food, water and shelter to make your bug out bag complete. These items can make all the difference in your survival chances.

To dig in the ground, you will need a folding shovel. This is necessary to dig a firepit, break up debris, snow, or rubble, and to bury waste.

A multi-tool is also essential. It can be used for many purposes. You will never be without this essential tool. A multi-tool with fine tools such as a tweezer, a toothpick and scissors is a must-have. These multi-tools are extremely useful. Most multi-tools will include a fil, saw, and a cutting knife, so you can handle many tasks.

A survival knife is an essential tool for any man.

While personal hygiene products should be kept at a minimum, they should still be used during the 72-hour period. You will need enough to last you three days. These items can be kept in smaller containers than the big bottles or tubes you normally keep in your bathroom.

It is essential to have a first aid kit with you in case of an emergency. The basic list includes plasters of different sizes, eyewash, blood clot, sterile wipes, and plasters.

If you depend on prescription drugs for your daily functioning, it can be difficult.

You should ensure that you have enough to last you at all times.

First, you could buy a pre-assembled first aid kit and then add the items you require. Many people prefer to make their own first aid kits. They can have more items, better quality, and can be much more specific.

It's possible that you will need things such as insect spray, painkillers, and sun lotion.

You should always have at least two foil survival blankets in your bag of tricks. It can be used to provide warmth or as part of first aid in case someone is in shock.

It's worth packing an axe, along with a knife. Many bushcrafters and survivalists prefer to carry an axe rather than a knife. They consider it a more versatile tool. This axe is more useful for clearing obstacles or getting through areas. It also doubles as a hammer that you can use to smash things out of the way.

Tape that can be used for sealing any leaks in a backpack or tent is a good option. Duct tape is the best choice because it has many other uses. It can seal a broken cup or repair a shoe. There are many other first aid uses.

Always bring a torch. It shouldn't be a cheap one. It should have a range of settings from low to maximum beam, as well as strobe and SOS functions. When you need light for reading and searching, the candlelight setting is perfect. SOS is extremely useful and worth the investment. The strobe function can be used to disorient people and signal them to get out of trouble.

For rechargeable batteries, you'll need batteries or solar-powered. This will ensure that your batteries never run out. You can also carry a solar charger for your other gear, such as a wind-up radio. These wind ups can also charge phones or batteries.

A wind up/solar radio is another essential. It is the only way you will know what is happening in other places. Information is the king, and you should be able tune into any station to get it. You may need to change your route if you don't know what is happening.

A wind up/solar radio can be small and lightweight, as well as being very affordable. Many solar-powered radios can be used to charge phones.

You will need a new set of supplies if you're traveling as a family with children or babies.

Travel time may be longer if you are on foot. Children are unable to move as fast as adults, so they may need more rest stops. Babies will need more frequent feedings.

Your bug out plans must include babies and young children. It can be difficult to manage a small child. However, a 10 year old should be able to pull their weight and make a contribution to the family.

Remember that rules may not be followed in a SHTF scenario. The easiest target for anyone who is hungry for food and water is a child. This brings me to the next point. How can you defend yourself and your family against bug out?

You've got an axe and a knife, which is probably all you will need for the first staggers of SHTF in the UK.

If you plan well and choose the 'optimum' time for bugging out, then everyone will still be trying to survive in those early stages.

You are not the only one who would have survived the SHTF and disaster effects. This 'window to opportunity' will make it easier for people to get from A-B.

There are people out there who would not hesitate to rob you or attack you. Situations like SHTF can lead to lawlessness and human greed. If you are able to remove yourself from this equation and set distance between yourself, the masses and these "disturbed" people, you'll encounter far fewer of them.

My personal opinion is that you might be forced to fight for supplies or you may have to leave your place. It is important to have a plan in place to ensure that you can defend yourself against attack.

A simple gesture of holding a knife or an axe is enough to signal to an attacker that you are willing to fight.

Chapter 19: How many bug out bags do you need?

Some people are not prepared for this area. A bug out bag is essential for you. You also need one for each member of your family, or anyone else who will be bugging you.

It is understandable that everyone's needs may differ from yours. They have to do their part and ensure that they have enough for bug out. There's always the possibility of the party being split up.

The bags should have similar survival items. All bags should have water filter, food, shelter, and clothing. If you are considering splitting up your family, communication becomes a problem. A simple walky-talky system can be a great option.

You may need to share your supplies with smaller children. Even the smallest child can still carry something if they can walk at the same pace as the rest of the group. A lightweight, small rucksack can carry a tarp and maybe some clothes. This will give the smallest child the feeling of being an integral part of the group.

You will face the exact same situation if you travel with elderly people who are unable to take care of their own needs. The elderly, while more difficult than your younger children, will in some ways be your greatest Achilles heel.

Frailty and exhaustion will strike much sooner than any family member.

This is something you should plan for. It is a good idea to stay with an elderly person, walk at their own pace, and have a little more gear in their backpack to protect them. The main group continues on to the final Bug Out location.

Get your Meet-Up Plan ready

It is one thing to know that you will need your bug out bag. It's another to have a place to meet. Both of these should be planned for. This is an important aspect of your preparations.

You must know where you are going when you make a plan. A meet-up plan requires a first destination, also known as a rally point. This is where everyone will meet.

Communication problems can make it impossible to know where everyone is, or if they are okay. This is why you should always have your Bug Out Bag and walky-talkies with you. You can get a decent walky-talky for as low as PS50 and will give you a range of 5-8 miles (in the open). These are highly recommended.

Everybody must agree on a rally point. This is important because if SHTF happens, it could be very easy for you to lose your loved ones. The agreed rally point is the only way for everyone to find one another again.

This will make it easier to know where to go. This is evident in news events from

174

third world countries if you pay attention to the news.

Families have had to flee their homes from man-made and natural disasters. The chaos caused the families to become separated on the way to safety.

Parents separated children from their parents. Sisters and brothers were split. You need a rally point to keep your family together. Even if you feel lost or overwhelmed, a rally point can help to keep you connected, even if it is a temporary situation.

It is important to understand how you will get there.

Many people will take their family car, or if they have prepared, they're Bug Out Vehicle. You'll be stuck if you use another mode of transport to get to work such as carpooling or taking the train. It is important to know how you are going to bug out.

Your plan could be that you take the car home - or, better, an off-road vehicle if it is necessary. You'll take the train if you are at work.

Always have a backup plan. You must be able to identify what next step should you take if your car doesn't start, or the train stops running. You should always have another option in case your first mode of transport is unavailable.

It is good to have a plan, and to know exactly where and how you will get there. It is not a good idea to practice the plan but never do a test run. A bug out plan, just like a fire drill should be practiced by all.

You'll be able see potential problems for your family and friends if you have a bug-out plan. These are important to know before you use the plan.

It is a great way to test your communications.

These devices can be used as a way to make sure you are always aware of what is happening while you try to reach the rally point. You can, for example, get information about a blocked road to your family members so they can choose another route.

You can travel from the rally point to any destination you choose if you and your family members meet up at it. A second rally point is just as important as a second destination. This is a smart way to have a plan B for when your plan A fails.

Strategy for a Long-Term Survival Program

Although it is possible to hope that an SHTF situation will not last too long, sometimes it works out that it will. You need a plan to ensure that you and your loved ones are able to survive, no matter how long it takes.

To ensure your safety, there are several areas you should focus on. First, you need to consider your food supplies. It is important to ensure that you have enough food for everyone and that your food storage facilities are as efficient as possible.

Some foods will keep well while others may not. It is important to understand the differences and be prepared to keep the right foods in your pantry. It is important to be able to manage your supplies and ensure that nothing spoils.

Start by ensuring you have enough dry foods. These are commonly considered to be your primary food list. You'll also find flour on this list. Both white and wheat flour are required.

You should store both baking soda and yeast. For nutrition, grains are good. There are many grains you can choose from, including wheat, barley and cornmeal as well as oats, rice, and oats. Grains are versatile and can be used in many ways. They are also nutritious and filling.

Dry pasta must be stored in large bags that are big enough to hold a family of four. These pasta are easy to prepare and can be enjoyed by all members of your family.

Beans and peas are essential. You should also make sure you have plenty of quick and easy fix foods. These include instant noodles, macaroni, instant potatoes and all kinds of packaged or boxed spaghetti that require only water.

These items will be used to flavor the food. These include sauces, seasonings, salt, pepper, and seasonings. Both sweet seasonings like cinnamon and regular seasonings like garlic will be needed.

Honey and cocoa powder are also good options. You should also have dried milk as a staple. Dry fruits make a great storage food. You can leave behind jam, jelly and preserves.

You can store protein bars and breakfast bars for many years. They are quick and easy to store for years. You can get a variety of flavors.

Sugar and oils are required. You will need a variety of oils. They will usually last for many years. You should have peanut butter and a variety nuts. These are both high in protein.

Stock up on a variety of cereals. Make sure you have plenty of popcorn. However, make sure to buy whole kernel popcorn so that you can use it with your oil. Make sure you have enough tea. Because the children love orange flavoured powder, some families like to stock up on it.

Make a large stock of canned goods. You should have a large stock of canned goods that will keep for many years. Tuna, as well as other meats, can be used to heat and eat various pastas, stews, and fruits and vegetables. Cans last for many years if kept out of direct sunlight in a dry, cool place. Some canned foods have a standard shelf life of 3 years. Honey and other natural foods like honey will not spoil.

If the SHTF situation continues, your food supply will eventually run out. You will need to find a way of replenishing your food. You should also save seeds for planting.

These food items could be grown while you are using your survival supplies. You can be prepared for whatever you need. You can preserve the food as it ripens and also use the seeds to plant new plants.

You must take care to protect the food you have saved for emergency survival. You must protect the food from light.

Food can be affected by the light. So can moisture. Pests can also be a problem. You should keep the food in a dark, cool place that isn't damp.

Keep pests away by sealing food in airtight containers. You can purchase storage containers specifically made for long-term food storage.

You need to remember two things when it comes to caring for your survivalist food stock. The first is to be aware of what you have. You'll lose track of what you have if you start to set aside food items.

The best way to stay on top of what you have is to create a master list. This will include every item and the amount you have.

You must also rotate food to ensure they are safe. You should keep canned goods that have an expiration date four years in the future, so that if the time goes by and there is no SHTF, you can put those foods in your current meal plan.

You can then simply take what you have with you to the store and replace it with what you need. Water is an essential part of any long-term strategy to ensure your survival.

Water can be stored in a variety of ways, so it will last for years and still taste good. You should always keep water in the original container that you bought it.

You don't want to risk contaminating your water supply by moving it to a bigger container. You must keep any stored water out of the sunlight.

Direct sunlight can cause temperature changes in water that can lead to bacteria growth.

Water that has good filtering is safe to drink. To be safe, however, it is a good idea to disinfect the water before using it.

To ensure safe drinking water, you can put the collected water in a good-sized container. Rainwater can be captured from your roof via your gutter.

Instead of letting the water run onto the ground, place a container with a lid underneath it. You will still need to use purification tablets, even if you take great care in storing your water supply.

There are many places where you can buy water test kits that will let you know if your water needs to be filtered.

A long-term shelter is an important part of your long-term survival plan.

These shelters can replace a temporary shelter such as a tent. When it comes to building shelters, nature has plenty to offer. You have many options: straw, rocks, stones, mud, and trees.

There are many factors to consider when it comes to long-term survival shelters. These include location, size, and money. It is a huge commitment to make an investment in a long-term shelter.

The biggest problem is where to actually put your bug-out location. If you are lucky enough to have land suitable for building a survival shelter, but the virus is already invading the nearby village.

It's a bit extreme, I know, but it is possible.

Everybody watches these amazing 'Doomsday" programs on TV. They show us underground bunkers and personalized fortresses. In reality, however, one must be both committed to the idea and rich to create a doomsday scenario.

Even bugging relatives miles away can help you get through. It is worth making a plan with family members or friends who are interested in being a bug-out location.

You may be able to live off the land if you've acquired the skills. However, it requires a lot of bushcraft skills to survive on your own. It's possible for one person to do it all on their own. However, a family of children will need to be familiar with the outdoors and how to live in these extremes.

This is not a happy family camping trip. I recommend that you actually try it during your bug-out practice drills, especially if it takes you a few days to get into the swing of things. I can tell you that it is not for the faint-hearted.

Hunting tools:

Hunting tools are essential for your long-term survival. These tools can be used to defend yourself as well. These tools can also be used for defense.

Weapons can be used to catch and bring in food. You can use weapons to make people think twice about attacking you. Weapons can also be used to defend yourself against an attack.

I recommend that you obtain a shotgun certificate or fire arms certificate to allow you to purchase, own, and keep a firearm at your house. Remember, in a SHTF situation, the Rule Of Law A Order is likely to go out the window so you'll have a strong weapon on you.

As it stands now, in the UK, owning a firearm on the firearms lists means that you will have to go through a lot of police investigations about your ability to possess such weapons. However, this is quite possible for most people.

You must have a weapon certificate that permits you to possess a rifle in order to bug out.

A 'full-on' firearm is not always the best option in a survival situation. Many weapons are capable of both defense and food procurement.

These weapons can be legally purchased and owned in the UK without the need for a license.

Bow (recurve, compound)

Crossbow (recurve, compound)

Catapults with high power

Air rifles (up to 12ft.lb).

These weapons are ideal for hunting small game such as rabbits, pheasants, and other birds. Larger animals such as deer can be taken down by a high-powered bow or crossbow.

Remember, you'll need bushcraft skills to butcher, cook, and field dress the meat if you are hunting for food. You must eat the meat immediately if you don't have a way to store it. This is why hunting smaller game.

There are other ways to get your food. You can use a fishing net and a fishing tool. These are lightweight and compact, but they can yield a lot of food. Fishing is the most efficient and simple method of hunting food.

You can set up a simple trap in a river with a net and let it 'fish for itself while you do other chores. It is quick and easy to gut fish. Fish are also very nutritious and easy to cook. A fishing kit is a great investment.

Do not forget to use a few basic snares. Nothing fancy, just fine wire or heavy-duty fishing line. To do this correctly, you will need to be proficient in trapping.

What you like and are most comfortable with will determine what you pack.

Many hunting tools can double as defense weapons. It doesn't have to be a fully automatic high-carbine rifle or handgun. Any of these would work to protect you from an attacker, looter, or simply to steal your supplies.

Conditioning yourself is a great way to be more aware of what's around you and who it is. Situation awareness is another important survival skill that is often overlooked. Preppers should learn it and practice it.

You will be able to prevent an attack from happening and will have the upper hand. An attacker will not hesitate to use a basic weapon to increase their awareness.

Many attacks are crimes of opportunity. Having a weapon can help deflect the crime from getting started.

Knives can be used as weapons or survival tools. Fixed blade knives are much more versatile and can be used to make dangerous situations. . A knife that is easy to carry should be attached to your belt, or tied to your leg. A knife is a sign that you are serious about business.

You can also use some other items as weapons. Spears should not be overlooked. These can be used for fishing, but they can also be used as weapons if necessary.

Bow and arrow can easily kill people so they are great weapons for keeping them at distance or, if necessary, stopping them from getting close.

You can use almost any object that packs a punch as a weapon. You can use them as weapons, such as baseball bats, or canes made from tree limbs.

Hunting tools and defense weapons go hand-in-hand, so keep that in mind when packing your rucksack.

Conclusion

Thank you again for downloading this book!

I hope this book was able to help you see how important emergency preparedness is to you and your family.

There is a great deal of information flooding the internet as of late about prepping for survival. Some people are turned off by a lot of the doomsday scenarios that are being tossed around and choose to ignore the subject altogether. You don't have to be one of the growing members of population who are preparing to survive some disaster that is likely to never occur in your lifetime. However, you can learn a lot of really valuable information that can be applied to your life today. Preparing to live through a natural disaster should be taken seriously. They do happen and they do seem to be increasing in frequency as well as strength. With so many people living in areas where disasters are likely to occur, it just makes sense to have a supply of food and water on hand in case you can't run to the store.

There is also the issue of our somewhat unstable economy. Most Americans are only a single paycheck away from total financial devastation. By keeping a supply of food on hand, you will rest easy knowing your family will have food to eat if you lose your job or suffer a major financial setback. Being able to focus your budget on things like the mortgage and electricity will help keep you going until you find a new job or you pull out of your financial slump.

You don't need to run out and max out your credit card today trying to create an instant emergency disaster kit. This is something that takes time. Adding a few extra cans of veggies to your normal grocery shopping list to put in your food storage softens the blow a bit.

Good luck to you and happy prepping!

9 781774 851210